INSIGHT *POCKET* GUIDES

KT-394-692

KaThManDu
Bikes & Hikes

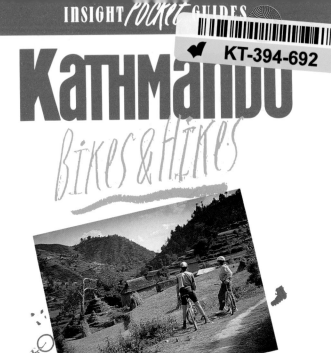

Written and Presented by **James Giambrone**

James Giambrone (signature)

INSIGHT
POCKET
GUIDES

Insight Pocket Guide:

Kathmandu
Bikes & Hikes

Directed by
Hans Höfer

Managing Editor
Lisa Choegyal

Edited by
Linda Kentro & Wendy Brewer Lama

Photography by
**James Giambrone,
Thomas L. Kelly & others**

Design Concept by
V. Barl

Design by
Karen Hoisington

© 1994 APA Publications (HK) Ltd

All Rights Reserved

Printed in Singapore by
**Höfer Press (Pte) Ltd
Fax: 65-8616438**

Distributed in the UK & Ireland by
GeoCenter International UK Ltd
The Viables Center, Harrow Way
Basingstoke, Hampshire RG22 4BJ
ISBN: 9-62421-552-9

Worldwide distribution enquiries:
Höfer Communications Pte Ltd
38 Joo Koon Road
Singapore 2262
ISBN: 9-62421-552-9

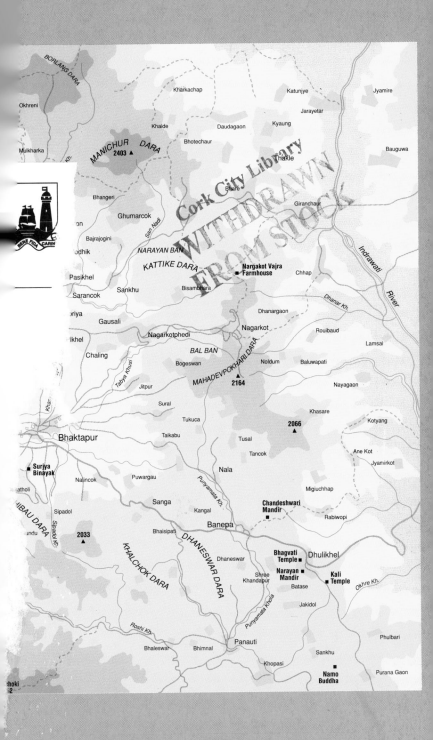

Follow me!

James Giambrone

When I first came to Kathmandu over 20 years ago, I had no idea it would capture my heart and offer a sense of home like no other. I still feel the original seduction — the sylvan valley of hidden gods and temples — but when the traffic and crowds get too much it is easy to revive that charm by hopping on my bike and heading out of town.

I've focussed on travel by mountain bike or foot because this is how the Kathmandu Valley's rich condensation of diverse terrain and cultural sites is best experienced. Small enough to become familiar but varied enough to get lost in, the Kathmandu Valley is a blend of playground and museum. The villages are not intended for motor traffic. In some places, you will encounter a perpetual gridlock of push-carts, rickshaws, buses, cars and motorcycles and an astonishing menagerie of farm animals. There is no better way to get around than by bicycle or foot, along routes not frequented by visitors but known to the Nepalese for thousands of years.

As a trek leader and initiator of the bike club Gear Wallahs (one who rides a many-geared bike), I've introduced my favourite bike and hike routes to many over the years. With this expertise I planned your itineraries, beginning with three full-day biking tours. These cover the essential sights of the four ancient kingdoms, the holy hill of Changu Narayan, the golden roofs of Pashupatinath, the sacred stupa at Bodhnath and two classic off-road rides through forest and farmland.

Eight bike options take you up wooded slopes and to secluded temples in remote pockets of the Valley, plus three longer overnight routes for a taste of greater Nepal. Likewise, eight half and full-day hikes lead you along ancient trails linking village and shrine while two more ambitious hikes extend to the valley rim and beyond, along routes of historic and mythical significance.

Nepal is a delicate place where imbalance leaves its mark. Just remember: walk and leave no footsteps; ride softly on the trails with an open heart.

Namaste— Welcome!

Contents

Preceding pages:
the imposing Swayambhunath stupa

Practical Information

Maps

Following pages:
Nepalese village girls

In the mid-1970s, a few adventurers rode old one-speed bikes at breakneck speeds down fire trails on California's Mount Tamalpais and gave birth to 'mountain biking' in America. Soon they started experimenting – adding gears, refining brakes and welding their own frames – and created prototypes of the mountain bike we use today, also known as the ATB or all-terrain bike.

Himalayan Mountain Biking

In 1983, the Himalayan Mountain Bike Expedition to Mount Everest initiated the sport in Nepal with a spectacular show. Craig Moffet and Brad Grunewald arrived with the first production-made mountain bikes. They reached as far as Kala Pattar 5,545m (18,192ft) where they recorded their feat. Few have been tempted to test mountain bike against mighty Himalaya peak again.

It was the call of the wide steppes of Tibet, with their opening in the mid-1980s, that incited the real fervour of bike activity in Kathmandu. Enthusiasts flew with their bikes from Hong Kong into the Tibetan capital city of Lhasa, toured the area, and then set out for the gruelling two-week journey over 5,181-m (17,000-ft) passes to Nepal. Word quickly spread of the wind and dust of Chinese truck caravans, the spartan accommodation, the challenges of pedalling down high passes into fierce headwinds and the great re-

Mammoth and machine in Kathmandu city

Contemplating Kakani

lief of reaching Nepal. It was the recuperation and rides in the Kathmandu Valley that won most praise in the end.

Biking in Kathmandu

Often, these early adventurers ended their trips trading their bikes for carpets, *thangkas* (religious paintings) or a ticket home, thus establishing a local stock of bikes. Expatriates first picked up on this perfect means of locomotion in the Valley, to the wonder of local inhabitants who marvelled at the 'pedalled motorcycles' that could climb up mountains, jump curbs and ride the roughest streets in Kathmandu without bending a rim or getting a flat.

Perhaps the hill to Patan was where mountain bikes captured the Nepalis' attention most persuasively. Every evening, hundreds of bicycle commuters going home pushed their single-speed Chinese and Indian made bikes uphill. When they saw foreigners sitting on

their bikes and pedalling uphill with ease it was love at first sight. Soon, Nepalis started importing inexpensive versions and the mountain bike business took off with sales to locals and rentals to tourists. Two shops opened exclusively renting ATBS.

In autumn 1991, Himalayan Mountain Bikes, which was founded in 1988, sponsored the first 3-day Fat Tire Festival culminating in an exciting 56-km (35-mile) race across the Kathmandu Valley rim. The Kakani itinerary (*Bike Itinerary 7*) describes the route which was won by a Nepali in an incredible 1½ hours. Today, more and more locals and foreigners are choosing mountain bikes as a convenient means for getting around town as well as exploring the Valley countryside.

Sun rays light the Valley from Nage Gompa

Biking Options

Nepal has innumerable biking options for bikers of varying ability. *Bike Itineraries 1–8* are half-day, full-day and overnight rides designed to experience the Valley. The overnight *Bike Itineraries 9–11* take you further afield and are for those who have combed the sites of the Valley, or who are itching to stretch their legs on a longer ride. Ride the whole trip or arrange for a lift for some sections. The overnight rides are just three of the countless dirt back roads to explore in Nepal. They are more difficult than the half and full-day trips and should only be undertaken by experienced bicyclists.

You can also combine other activities by riding out to your trekking trailhead or by interspersing a long ride with river rafting. Never take your bike on tourist trekking trails; grades are often dangerously steep, with long stretches of stairs, and paths are often shared with unwary livestock and villagers. Biking on roads is best minimised because of heavy truck traffic. To help you plan your rides, I have given biking distances and times for each ride. Preparation is critical for the longer trips. Not only must your bicycle be in top form but mind and body should also be ready to endure what may seem like endless uphills or unfair flat tyres in the heat of the midday sun. I encourage the occasional push-to-your-limit approach but not for hundreds of kilometres.

Being out of shape on these long hauls of course invites problems; and to enjoy the experience, train hard, drink sufficient water and test yourself well before the trip. Unless you are an inveterate independent cyclist, I recommend doing the longer trips with a professional bike tour operator. Himalayan Mountain Bikes (see *Practical Information*) operates biking expeditions in and around the Valley. It is a reliable company whose services include lodging, food and a guide who doubles as a translator and mechanic.

Hiking Options

Not everyone has the time or the energy to trek deep into the Himalaya; if so the half- and full-day *Hike Itineraries 12–19* will suffice. The overnight *Hike Itineraries 20* and *21* into the Kathmandu Valley hills are more arduous and introduce village life, even wilderness, in a short time. Unless you are a veteran trekker, I recommend that you go with a reputable trekking agent in Kathmandu for guide and support services. It frees you to relax and enjoy the experience. If you are determined to backpack, however, be sure to take along a buddy as hiking alone is never wise.

Hikes are estimated in terms of hours, following the logic that elevation gain and loss usually overshadows distance as a measure of energy and time required. The times are moderate and your own may fluctuate considerably, depending on your speed and sightseeing interests. The treks are ideal for spring and fall when skies are clear and trails are free of mud and leeches. Between November and February, be prepared for freezing temperatures at night and heavy intermittent rain from mid-June to early September.

Right: biking the curves to Kakani

Day it

Day ①

Kathmandu, Swayambhunath and Teenpipli

Biking Distance: 24km (15 miles); Biking Time: 3–4 hours

This first day's outing will take you from hubbub to hush. Start in the heart of old Kathmandu, which is happily congested with merchants, temples and cows. Wind your way up to holy Swayambhunath, encountering monks and monkeys at the oldest and most important Buddhist temple in Kathmandu Valley. Take a break for lunch at the Vajra Hotel and then ride up and over the Valley rim, re-entering at the northwest corner through terraced farmland and villages lost in time.

Starting out on your bike in front of **Nepal Grindlays Bank** on Kantipath, head south toward **Rani Pokhari**, the Queen's Pond. Prepare to leave the exhaust-filled 20th century by turning right into a crowded lane. Pass through 'Little Bangkok', with the latest Western fashions from Thailand. Note 'bicycle corner', home to Nepal's retail bike and spare parts market.

The lane explodes into **Asan Tole**, 1,000-year-old home to a swirl of Nepali merchants, farmers and gods. A large vegetable market, set up early each morning, swarms with equally exotic shoppers. In the temple to your left, the goddess Annapurna, protector of harvests and nourishment, watches over her favourite domain.

They say that everyone in

Rani Pokhari – the Queen's Pond

19th century Durbar Square lithograph

Nepal eventually passes through Asan Tole and a single day probably sees the passage of at least one representative of each of the 37
major ethnic groups.

Let the crowd sweep you along the main lane (exiting southwest)
under ornate woodcarved balconies. Plastic wares and curio shops
indicate that this remains a main artery for local shopping. On the
right you will see an exquisitely carved octagonal **Krishna Shrine**
covered with fine Newari woodcarving. Next is **Tilang Ghar**, with
78 rifle-carrying soldiers painted on the walls, and famous for being the first building after the royal palace to use glass.

Just before Kel Tole on the right you pass a small well-propor-
tioned temple called **Lunchen Lun Bun Ajima** whose entrance is below today's ground level due to centuries of subsidence.

To your right, two griffins protect the inner sanctum of the temple of **Seto Machhendranath**, the guardian deity of Kathmandu.
Unfortunately, its lower portion is covered with iron lattice due to
past plundering of its sculptures by art thieves, but this does not
diminish the beauty of its form, crowned by a graceful double-
tiered roof. This Buddhist site also houses a *vihar*, one of the few
Newari Buddhist monasteries still standing in the Valley. The central shrine is surrounded with *chaityas* (stupas) and stone pillars

The dense and diverse commerce of Indra Chowk

supporting some exquisite Newari metal statuary. This shrine is devoted to Padmapani Lokiteshwar, a form of Avalokiteshwara, (God of Compassion) whose image adorns the temple in 108 forms. The paintings are by Nepal's most famous artist, Siddhimuni Sakya. During the night old men come here to sing *bhajan* (religious songs).

Leave the courtyard through a small walkway opposite the entrance, pass by the **pottery market**, turn right and make your way to the main road again, alongside the sunken temple.

Past stacks of copper water pots you reach **Indra Chowk**, with piles of wool shawls for sale on the temple tiers. On the left, between buildings, is a small alley leading to the **bead market** – a kaleidoscope of glitter where you can make up necklaces, a sure winner for gifts. The Hindu god, Akash Bhairav sits in his second floor temple and is also nightly serenaded with *bhajan*. During the festival of **Indrajatra** (August–September) he is brought out for public view, festooned with garlands and plied with food.

From Indra Chowk angle southwest to **Makhan Tole** where **Taleju Bhawan** dominates the skyline on your left over a series of shops selling inexpensive *thangkas*. On your right stands a recently excavated stone image from the 8th century. Here begins the **Kathmandu Durbar Square** complex, the buildings that comprise the oldest extant **Royal Palace** site.

Krishna Shrine

You are not allowed to enter Taleju Bhawan unless you are a Hindu but you can wander with your bike amongst these living monuments of historical rulers. Follow the flagstone path to a huge statue of Black Bhairav, revered as a form of Shiva, on the left and a pair of large drums high up to the right. It was to Bhairav, in front of the police headquarters, that suspected thieves were brought for interrogation – a common belief that those who lied would die. The drums are rung to ward off evil spirits during the festival of Degu Taleju. Just past the Bhairav statue behind the large lattice screen is an enormous mask of Sweta Bhairav.

Turn left and enter the **Hanuman Dhoka Durbar** (open 10am–4pm, closed Tuesday) and **Nasal Chowk**, the King Tribhuvan museum. The four towers commemorate the unification of Nepal in the 18th century. After the victory of King Prithvi Narayan Shah, each of the four conquered kingdoms designed and built a tower, all of which still stand today, thanks to a UNESCO project in the early 1970s. **Basantapur Tower** has nine stories, **Kirtipur Tower** has a domed copper roof, the **Bhaktapur Tower** is octagonal and the classic **Lalitpur Tower** overlooks New Road. You can walk up Basantapur Tower for a magnificent view over the city.

Kasthamandap

Re-enter the flagstone road and walk 20m (66ft) left into Durbar Square, surrounded by magnificent temples and the old Royal Palace. Starting from straight ahead; clockwise you see the 17th-century **Trailokya Mohan Temple** dedicated to Krishna, at the 2 o'clock position the 17th-century **Manju Deval** dedicated to Shiva and on the immediate right a temple dedicated to the lovers Shiva and Parvati, peering out of the upper story window.

Beyond the big temples the route opens onto **Maru Tole**, home to **Kasthamandap**, the large wooden building on your right. Legend says that it was made entirely from one single tree and that this famous building spawned the name Kathmandu. Circle it from the left side. Note the small **Ganesh Temple** on your left just before the square. Go east, passing **Kumari Bahal** on your right where the Living Goddess resides. The road opens into **Basantapur Square**, previous home of the Royal Elephants and now a curio bazaar well worth a browse.

On the left is the dominating Hanuman Dhoka complex. Just be-

Trinkets for sale in Basantapur

yond Basantapur Square is the famous **Freak Street** where hippie travellers hung out in the 1960s and early 1970s. It was abandoned when shopkeepers left en masse for Thamel in the late 1970s. Nowadays, Freak Street quietly awaits its next incarnation.

Proceed straight on to **New Road** (also called Ganga Path), so named after the reconstruction that followed the devastating earthquake of 1934. Across from the Crystal Hotel is the **Supermarket** with escalator and underground parking. This area is the prime shopping centre for imported goods, jewellery and stationery.

New Road ends at **Tundhikhel**, the parade ground for all regal and civic ceremonies. Turn left. On your right is the very well-attended Buddhist temple of **Mahakala**, protector of the land. Continue straight back 500m (1,640ft) to Grindlays Bank where you started.

Take the next turn left at the large roundabout. Pass one intersection; turn left where the street opens into an enlarged T-intersection. You are heading toward **Thahiti Tole**. Stop and lock up your bike for an art tour of traditional paintings at **Indigo Gallery** (Tel: 220634). The gallery represents Nepal's most talented *thangka* painters and has the best collection in Kathmandu.

Leave the Gallery, head left and turn first right, heading towards Chetrapati on your bike. Continue on to **Chetrapati 'bandstand'**, a charming wrought-iron centrepiece that looks like it should be jumping with drums, horns and parasols. Standing with your back to the door of the small, two-tiered Bhairav temple, turn left and make the first right. You are going towards Swayambhunath *stupa* (a bell-shaped relic chamber) immediately visible in the distance. Coast downhill to the Vishnumati River and the Hindu temple complex of **Indrainni**, one of eight Astha Matrika (mother goddess) temples in the Valley and a crema-

tion *ghat* for Hindus.

Across the river and on your right is the Buddhist temple dedicated to Bijeswari Bajra Jogini, one of the four most important mother goddess temples in the Valley. The road forks here; take the left fork and then a right up past the Hotel Vajra on your left. These roads are but wider lanes of asphalt laid over the ancient foot trails to Swayambhunath, compacted by millions of pilgrims over the years and still used by hundreds of daily worshippers.

At the top of the climb, turn left and start the approach to Swayambhunath. On a clear day you can see Nagarjun, Shivapuri and even Langtang Himal mountains to your right.

At the bottom of the main entrance stairway to the Swayambhunath hillock is a small stone *mandala* with the footprints of the Buddha. People may be prostrating and bowing their heads to them in reverence. If you are feeling energetic, lock your bike here and climb the 300-plus steps, the traditional approach to the temple and recommended as the most merit-gaining.

If you prefer a bikeable route, turn left and join the cortege of pilgrims doing *kora* – a circumambulation or holy circuit – always going clockwise. On your right are Tibetan buildings which enclose

huge prayer wheels, endlessly turning with the spins of devout Buddhists, disseminating their enclosed prayer 'Hail the Jewel in the Lotus'. This *mantra* is carved, printed or painted and sent into the wind wherever Tibetans reside.

It is believed that the symbolism of the sacred lotus follows its botanical parts. It is rooted in earth (our individual births), grows up through water (the vicissitudes of worldly existence), lays its leaf on the water and unfolds its blossom high in air untouched by earth or water (air symbolising purity). So we live like the lotus and the prayer is sent out to the universe for the benefit of all. Past the prayer wheels is the little village of Swayambhunath. To reach the top of the hill, turn right, stay right

Chetrapati 'bandstand'

The all-seeing eyes of the Swayambunath stupa

and follow the road up to a parking lot near the top. Lock your bike to the stair railing.

Swayambhunath, steeped in legend, is the oldest temple and settlement of the Kathmandu Valley. Eons ago, Buddha Vipssaya tossed a lotus seed into the lake that then filled the Valley and prophesied that a Self-Created one, Swayambhu, would emerge from this lake as a flame. Ages later, another Buddha, Visvabhu, prophesied that a Bodhisattva (Divine Being) would come and drain the lake. Lord Manjushri, Buddhist god of wisdom, who emanated as Visvakarma the Hindu god and builder of the universe, viewed the lotus afloat in the lake while meditating atop Nagarjun hill. Wishing it accessible to devotees, he cleft a gorge in the southern mountains to drain the lake. When the water was gone, the lotus was found resting atop Swayambhunath hillock and the Valley became habitable for people.

The Swayambhunath stupa is home to the five-Buddha family. Each Buddha image sits enclosed in an ornate *pukachin* (house of god) covered with gilded beaten copper. Bodhisattvas and protectors surround the image, while the attendant beast or vehicle sits below. Starting from the front of the 1½-m (5-ft) long *vajra*, or thunderbolt, at the top of the east-facing staircase in the *pukachin* sits Akshobhya, followed by Vairocana, the centre or Adi-Buddha. Ratnasambhava sits to the south, Amitabha in the west and Amoghasiddi in the north. The stupa and the Buddha family are worshipped daily but the major festival is **Buddha Jayanti** from April–May, celebrating the birth, enlighten-

Decked out in jewellery

ment and passing of Lord Buddha. On this day butter lamps are lighted and a special offering takes place at night.

The ornate gilded copper temple to the northwest of the stupa is for the Hindu god Harati Ajima, protector from smallpox. Its presence at a major Buddhist site is exemplary of the renowned Nepali religious syncretism. Beyond is the 2½m- (8ft-) tall 10th-century standing Buddha and farther down an enormous seated Buddha of the same period. Below and to the north is Shantipur, which is worshipped by the King during droughts. Before leaving the complex, visit the museum at the top of the steps to the parking area. Get back on your bike, go downhill and turn right, rejoining the circumambulation of the hillock.

Twenty-five years ago, the Flower Power generation chose the foot of Swayambhunath as its residence, adding its own flavour to the profusion of pilgrims. It was here that travellers first went into the restaurant kitchens of The Tibetan Brothers and Narko's and taught Nepalis the fine art of making French toast, brownies and apple pie. These were to be perfected by the likes of Vishnu's Pie and Chai, Aunt Jane's and the Unity Restaurant, heralded forerunners of today's thriving restaurant trade in this area.

Pilgrims' route to Swayambhunath

Heading west further along the paved road you will pass several Tibetan monasteries, the one on your left enclosing a huge revolving prayer wheel. Across the Ring Road intersection, marked by hundreds of prayer flags, look for the **Ani Gompa**, a Tibetan Buddhist nunnery. These nuns were twice exiled: first from Tibet and second when a flash flood destroyed their home in Helambu. Donations were collected and the proceeds used to build this monastery in 1989.

The road running west past the monastery will take you up and out of the Valley to Ichangu Narayan (see *Bike Itinerary 4*).

Continue your circumambulation and return to the front steps of Swayambhunath. Turn left and stop for lunch at the **Hotel Vajra,** a charming assemblage of Newari architecture. The rooftop garden bar is an excellent place for views, daytime or sunset. *Momos* (steamed meat or vegetable filled dumplings) are particularly good.

Monsoon clouds over Swayambhunath Hill

After a high-carbohydrate lunch and a piece of apple pie, head back to Swayambhunath but turn right onto a dirt road just before you reach the steps. Follow it down to Ring Road and turn right.

Continue north to the main Balaju intersection at the round-about. Turn left and go up to the Balaju bazaar. On the left is **Balaju Water Gardens** where I recommend a brief detour. For a one-rupee fee you can visit a temple which holds the 14th-century Shitala Mai, protector from smallpox. Of the many small sculptures sitting outside the temple, the most noteworthy is the 16th-century Harihari, a half-Vishnu, half-Shiva god. Next to the temple is the Licchavi stone sculpture of a re-clining Vishnu.

Beasts spewing water

Just below are the famous 22 water spouts – a line of or-derly beasts who, in good sea-son, spew forth jets of water into the fountain. On full moon in March–April, thousands of pilgrims come to celebrate **Lhuti Punbhi** by bathing here and climbing to the top of Nagarjun for religious ceremonies. This festival honours the Buddha Vipssaya.

Return to the entrance, go uphill to a T-junction and then straight. You are riding around the base of **Nagarjun**, also known as **Rani Ban** or Queen's Forest, one of the most densely forested ar-eas within close proximity of Kathmandu. This is the beginning of the only major climb on this ride, with an idyllic shady setting that will ease your effort. To your right, enjoy the changing scenes in this corner of the Valley: terraced rice paddies and mustard fields surrounding clusters of thatch-topped, ochre-mudded houses.

On the other side of this finger of the Valley you can see two roads that will be your return route. Soon you pass the main entrance gate to Nagarjun.

Further along you reach the Nagarjun saddle, beyond which are views of lush hillsides with the Kakani saddle in the distance framing a view of Ganesh Himal (7,150m/23,458ft). In the foreground of this panorama is a small pagoda pavilion, a great spot for a rest. To get there, take the dirt road on your left at the top of the first small hill past the Nagarjun saddle.

Just before the turn-off to the pavilion you will pass the entrance of the newly-opened **Osho Tapoban Forest Retreat Centre**, a renovated private residence owned by devotees of Rajneesh, a Tantric Hindu *guru*. This peaceful retreat welcomes casual visitors.

The road known to residents as the Kakani Road continues level until you reach the village of **Teenpipli**. Here you can fuel up on cookies and tea and perhaps have your first experience of being 'the circus that came to town' as the children crowd around to practise their English. Patience and a bit of humour go a long way.

The village's original name was Teenpipal which literally translates as 'three *pipal* trees' but a heavy storm has left only two of the traditional holy protectors standing. The beautiful, thick canopied *pipal* tree is venerated as having sheltered Buddha during his moment of enlightenment. The tree is planted for religious merit, usually paired with a *bahar* (banyan) tree, its 'wife', and surrounded by a stone seat called a *chautara*. These shaded rest-stops are appreciated by those carrying burdens and are popular local gathering places.

Teenpipli is identified by a sharp left turn with an immediate view of the Kathmandu Valley to your right. Leave the paved road by taking the dirt road beyond the *pipal* tree.

Plunge headlong into lush countryside

Villagers and bikers

Re-enter the Valley on a dirt road which contours the north-west foothills and overlooks the Valley. After 15 minutes, ignoring the main road down at Jitpurphedi, a walking trail turns right leading down to the Valley floor. The turn-off is identified in three ways; Mr Ram's tea shop on the right, a big boulder on either side of the road and the beginnings of an uphill grade.

Dismount and walk down 100m (328ft) to the bottom where you turn right. Pay special heed during the monsoon when the trail is a waterway. The trail soon merges with the rice fields. You will be a curiosity to the farmers who will wonder why you are biking over such rough terrain. You can respond to such queries with *'anande chha'* (it's very peaceful). A friendly, respectful attitude will assure you ready passage as trespassing is not a concept held in the village. Be prepared, however, for obstacles such as a buffalo being herded by a child, a farmer carrying his ancient wooden plough slung over his shoulder, an assortment of goats, dogs, ducks and what appears like moving haystacks. There are people under those haystacks walking at a brisk pace – give them right of way.

The Valley ride is mostly a descent from here. With careful at-

tention you can coast through the villages, politely tipping your helmet to farmer and school boy. Depending upon the season, you may see farm people engaged in the growing of rice, wheat or mustard. Family and friends gather to help plant or harvest each other's fields. Surrounded as you are by timeless farm life, it is difficult to believe that downtown Kathmandu and Nirula's 28 Flavours ice-cream shop are only about 30 minutes away!

Mother and child

The trail soon descends rapidly to the lip of a small gorge with vegetable fields below. You can see the saddle at Teenpipli to your right. Walk, do not attempt to ride the sections that are narrow trails or rice paddy bunds. It is beautiful along this small ridge-top path and besides being safer, walking will allow you a better look around. The trail crosses over to the left of the forest and down to another small valley. Walk the bike across this section until you reach **Dharmastali** village. Here, you could turn right to go directly back to Kathmandu or continue for another 30 minutes.

Continue and enter a typical mid-size Newari village. While older folks dry grains on mats lying on the road or build haystacks for winter fodder, small children play their favourite game — Driving the Car. This is played by running and rolling a wire hoop guided with a stick. They do this all over Nepal and when kids see a two-wheeled toy (your bike) rolling by, they cannot help but hang on to it and run alongside. They mean no harm but can cause drag or unbalance — unwanted experiences for a tired biker. Tell them *'na chhunee'*, meaning 'don't touch' in Nepali.

Follow the meandering trail towards **Khattekola**. Turn right at the next T-junction where **Bedigoth**, a Tamang village, sits on top of a wide plateau. Just past it, the trail drops down a roller coaster ride to the Valley floor and crosses a bridge. Again, do not ride but walk over this bridge.

The trail descends to the Mahadev Khola on the left. Cross it at **Jaranku** and join a well-travelled road heading towards

Ride past picturesque rice fields

Balaju. To your right looms Nagarjun mountain which you rode by a few hours ago. The road crosses the river but you stay on the left side and follow the path through a small village. Where the trail joins the main road, turn right and cross another bridge.

At the outskirts of Balaju, where you started your climb, turn left and coast downhill, and go left again onto Ring Road. You will soon cross the Vishnumati River. Turn right at the first paved road on your right. At the T-junction at the top of a short hill, turn left. Turn right at the next intersection and you are in downtown Kathmandu at the roundabout that leads to **Thamel**.

Finish this fantastic day with a hot shower and go for dinner at either **Himthai** (Tel: 529230) in Thamel for Thai food or to **Al Fresco** at the **Soaltee Oberoi** for pasta (Tel: 272550).

Day 2

Bhaktapur, Changu Narayan, Pashupatinath and Bodhnath

Biking Distance: 30km (18.6 miles); Biking Time: 4–5 hours

This all-day bike ride, with some exploration on foot, highlights some of the Valley's most important temples and settlements. Begin with traditional Thimi and the restored medieval capital of Bhaktapur. Gear down for a winding ascent to Changu Narayan Temple and return via farming villages. Take an unusual approach to Pashupatinath, popular among Lord Shiva worshippers and finish up at Bodhnath stupa, a centre of Tibetan Buddhism and momo-making (meat or vegetable dumplings).

Religious festival fills Taumadi Square, Bhaktapur

Bhaktapur with the Himalaya as a backdrop

Set off early from Kathmandu with a hearty packed lunch for a fun day of both tame terrain and daring exploration. Bring a bike lock so you can explore the temples on foot at ease. Follow the old road to Thimi and Bhaktapur. Leaving Thimi, the road heads due east for about 1km (½ mile), then curves right and crosses a small bridge. The first left beyond the bridge leads to Nagarkot; continue straight and turn left at the second road, and mount the hill flanked by a lovely pine forest into **Bhaktapur**.

Continue past army barracks, a parade ground and an old fire station with vintage trucks. The road jogs around **Siddha Pokhari**, a rectangular pond built in the 16th century. Its waters have never been emptied — legend has it that a large serpent dwells within and no Nepali dares enter the compound.

The road narrows between impressive carved wooden windows and you enter old Bhaktapur, also known as **Bhadgaon** or City of Devotees. The Newari people are farmers and traders; the women distinguished by their traditional black with red-bordered saris. Handicraft trades such as pottery, metal-working and wood-carving are still active.

Ride the main road through an enormous gateway to **Bhaktapur Durbar Square**. Of the Valley's three historic capitals, including Kathmandu and Patan, Bhaktapur's Durbar or Palace Square was the largest, boasting 99 royal courtyards and uncountable art masterpieces. A royal seat of power since the 9th and perhaps even 5th

Bhaktapur doorway of gold

Five-roofed Nyatapola Temple with stone guardians

century AD, Bhaktapur grew as each king built scores of monuments to gods and goddesses, beseeching victory in battle. However, this insurance policy did not seem to extend to natural disasters as many temples were destroyed in a 1934 earthquake.

Entering the square, dismount and walk your bike past the impressive stone sculptures of the 18-armed Ugrachandi Durga and 12-armed Bhairav, adorned with necklaces of severed heads.

On the left is **Sundari Chowk**, the royal ritual bathing courtyard. From the centre rises a large *naga*, a mythical snake. Continuing east, the **National Art Gallery** (open daily 10.30am–4pm, except Tuesday and holidays, entrance 50 paisa) is guarded by Hanuman the monkey-god and Narsingh the man-lion. The gallery has a fine collection of paintings and sculptures.

Next door, the **Sun Dhoka** or Golden Gate is perhaps the Valley's greatest masterpiece of Newari *repousse* art. Study the details, rich in Buddhist and Hindu images, recalling Nepal's successful syncretism of the two religions. Opposite the gleaming doors stands a stone pillar mounted by a statue of **Bupathindra Malla**, one of the great Malla kings of the 17th century.

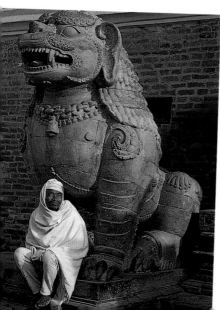

Lock your bike and enter the Golden Gate, passing through its inner courtyards to the **Taleju** and **Kumari chowks** (courtyards). Over the doorway is an exquisite example of the

Bhaktapur Durbar Square

half-circle *torana*, similar to that featured in wood or brass at many Valley temples. Unfortunately, these *chowks* are off-limits to non-Hindus, but with a little persuasion the guard may allow you a glimpse of the interior from the doorway.

Re-emerging at Durbar Square, look left towards the **Chaysiln Mandap**, an ocagonal pavilion recently rebuilt by Newari craftsmen with German financial support. Destroyed in the earthquake, a steel structure now braces the *mandap's* upper wooden floor, painstakingly carved in sections and pieced together without nails. Opposite stands the **Palace of 55 Windows** which in fact has only 53 windows as two were inadvertently forgotten in the reconstruction.

Heading south, away from the palace, notice the large 16th-century **Pashupati Temple** with its erotic relief.

Past the temple, exit Durbar Square left, pushing your bike down a narrow lane lined with souvenir shops. Emerge at **Taumadi Square** with the impressive five-roofed **Nyatapola Temple** dedicated to the Tantric goddess Siddhi Lakshmi. Five pairs of mythical and animal figures as well as solid stone Malla wrestlers guard it, one of only two five-roofed temples in the Kathmandu Valley (the other being Kumbeshwar in Patan). Standing 30m (98ft) high, it is the Valley's tallest temple.

Take the lane to the right from the Square's southwestern corner and turn left to reach the **Potters' Market** where hundreds of pots dry in the open square.

Return to Taumadi Square, cross to the far right corner and ride or walk up a bricked gradient. Follow the signs to **Dattatraya Square** – a 10-minute ride east along a busy shopping street. **Dattatraya Temple**, which serves both as a pilgrim shelter and com-

Dattatraya Temple at night

Handmade pottery drying in the sun

munity forum, stands in the middle of the square. To the right is **Pujari Math** (Priest's House) built in 1763, now containing a woodcarving museum (open daily 10.30am–4pm, except Tuesday and holidays, entrance 50 paisa). Its superbly carved windows deserve the same attention as the famous **Peacock Window** down the building's side alley.

From Dattatraya Square, continue easterly (away from Durbar Square) along the main street and take the first left turning to **Maha Durga Temple**, enjoying another 'off the beaten track' corner of Bhaktapur. The lane jogs left, then straightens out, descending north to the main road that bypasses Bhaktapur (the way to Nagarkot). Turn left, and watch out for a small sign on an electric pole pointing north to Changu Narayan. Ask anyone if you are unsure. Plan on 45 minutes' to an hour's ride to the temple on this steep but paved gradient.

Gaining elevation quickly, your pace slows to a snail's, and life drifts by: children shoot marbles across dung-plastered patios where leather-skinned women sit combing their long locks. Some 500 years ago, Bhaktapur thrived on the Valley's best agricultural land. Even now as you snake through seas of rice, wheat and corn, the extraordinary skills of the *jyapus*, a farmer caste, working with just an ox and plough are evident.

At last the road levels out and the magnificent Himalaya protrude behind the northern hills. Looking northeast, you see the honeycomb village of Sankhu and the Manohara River; looking south, Bhaktapur and the Hanumante River.

To reach **Changu Narayan Temple**, continue west along

Potters' Market, Bhaktapur

the ridge and carry your bike for five minutes up the steps through Changu Narayan village. Enter the temple compound through a small door and you step into a world like no other. Here, time seems to have stood still; half-animal, half-god figures peer from every corner and crevice. Some of the Valley's greatest masterpieces stand as humble reminders of the skilful artisans from millennia ago.

Changu Narayan Temple

Changu Narayan honours Lord Vishnu of the supreme Hindu trinity. Although the main structure was rebuilt as recently as 1702, many of the surrounding art pieces date to the 6th and 9th centuries during Licchavi times.

The stone **stele** standing on the west side opposite the robust Garuda and encased golden images of a Malla King and Queen, is said to be the earliest known inscription in the Kathmandu Valley, recounting King Manadeva I's military conquests of AD464. The exquisite stone tablet shows **Visvarupa**, aspect of Vishnu, with 10 heads and 10 arms standing amidst different levels of the universe.

Spend some time here taking in the rich imagery and perhaps a cup of tea from the local vendor. This is a good place for lunch, about midway on your tour. Return to Thimi either by the same way you came or try something new; a series of trails and dirt roads with a few carry-sections. This adventurous route exits the temple courtyard due west and descends two flights of stone steps to the first cluster of houses. Follow the stairs left, descending for a few minutes on foot.

Stay with the stairs until you see a break in the pine forest to the left. Mount and brake your way down the grassy hillside past building ruins. Stay right, straightening out towards the south.

Changu Narayan temple dates back to the 6th century

Golden roofs of Changu from afar

From the bottom, the trail is obvious, curving its way right and then left into a football size clearing shaded by a sprawling *pipal* tree. Pass the tree to the right and stay on the path as it takes you across a small valley and up a short steep section to a four-way junction marked by a water tower and another *pipal* tree.

Turning right, you pass a row of houses on the right and after 3–4 minutes, a school on your left. Reach another large clearing with a road exiting right; stay straight ahead, leaving the other way for another day.

It is an easy glide from here curving right, then left, generally heading south-easterly. Stay right, continuing for about 5–10 minutes, then at the T-intersection on a large flat field turn right and follow the dirt road due south for about 1½km (1 mile) to meet the old Thimi-Bhaktapur road where you passed this morning. If unsure, ask the way to Thimi.

Turn right, head towards Thimi and on to the Pepsi plant. Do not turn left to reach the highway (unless you are tired of trail riding), but head straight for the airport runway up a short climb and follow the dirt road north (right) around the perimeter. Airport guards will keep you on the right track and may even let you cross the runway if the coast is clear. (Which airport in the world would let you do that?) If so, exit the airport, turn right at Ring Road and just before the bridge take a right turn, following the banks of the Bagmati River into Pashupatinath.

Otherwise, stay on the airport's east side, skirting the landing field which was once known as **Gauchar** from the days when the airport was a cow pasture. The control tower still rings a siren to clear the runway of people, cows and mountain bikers. At the northern end, turn left and leave the dirt road and runway to follow a meandering trail towards the

Cultivated fields surround Bhaktapur

Pashupatinath temple

west, descending in 10–15 minutes of half-riding, half-pushing to a large football field on the southeast side of the Bagmati River. You can see the white dome of Bodhnath to the north.

Head towards the white **Guhyeshwari Temple** staying on the left bank of the river. Hindu devotees here worship the female emanation of Shiva, called Durga or Guhyeshwari, while Buddhists recognize the female power as Prajnaparamita.

Follow the paved road from the temple steps, crossing a bridge and curving left. Just beyond the bridge, notice a paved road to the right. You will return later and take this to Bodhnath.

But first a visit to **Pashupatinath** is a must, as it is for every Hindu at least once in a lifetime. One of the four primary Shiva worship sites of the subcontinent, here Shiva takes the identity of Pashupati, lord of the beasts, represented by the prolific *lingum* or phallus. The premier five-faced *lingum* is housed inside the gilded triple-roofed temple, to which only Hindus are permitted entry. Nonetheless, this is one of the most interesting sites in the Valley to many visitors and deserves a visit.

Turn left onto the main temple approach road. Leave your bike

Kathmandu Valley from Changu Narayan

locked at one of the shops outside the grounds. Enter the gate and cross the bridge over the sacred Bagmati River and climb the steps of the temple for an overview. On the opposite side are cremation *ghats* often in use. For Hindus, to die and be cremated on the banks of the Bagmati, tributary to the holy Ganges River, as to bathe and perform purification rites in these waters, is considered beneficial in attaining freedom from the incessant cycles of rebirth.

This is a place you may want to return to early in the morning when the waters' mist lends an eerie air, or perhaps during Shivaratri, usually in February–March, when thousands of *sadhus* (holy men) gather to perform amazing feats of yoga, demonstrating their dedication to Lord Shiva, the creator and destroyer.

And now on to Bodhnath, centre of Kathmandu's Tibetan community, before heading home. Allow at least 1½ hours of easy riding and sightseeing. Retrace your tyre tracks towards Guhyeshwari but turn left before the bridge. As the paved road turns to dirt and curves to the right, continue straight on a narrower path which soon leads to the main Bodhnath road. It's a bit rough so you may want to walk. Turn right onto a busy thoroughfare and reach the decorated archway to **Bodhnath Stupa** on the left in about 10 minutes.

Since its construction at least 1,400 years ago, pilgrims from all parts of Buddhist Asia have

Devotee circumambulates Bodhnath

been circling Bodhnath. Join the motley parade of Tibetans, Sherpas, Bhutanese, Ladakhis and even the occasional Thai or Japanese monk as they circle the huge stupa in a clockwise direction, twirling hand-held prayer wheels or spinning the mounted ones.

Tibetan mask

Like every *stupa*, Bodhnath's design represents each of the five natural elements, also reflected in the five coloured flags. The stepped base is shaped like a *mandala* (sacred diagram). Inside the white-washed dome, splashed with saffron in the shapes of lotus blossoms, are precious relics. The eyes looking in four directions, as at Swayambhunath, represent compassion while the 'third eye' symbolises wisdom. The nose, appearing like a question mark, is the Nepalese number one, *ek*, for unity. The 13 golden steps symbolise the path toward *nirvana*, or enlightenment, topped by forms representing air and ether. Prayer flags are strung to all corners.

Interrupt your circumambulation to mount the *stupa* steps on the northern side. How many gilded roofs of monasteries can you see from the upper tier? Probably at least two dozen. You are welcome to visit them but enter discreetly, leaving shoes outside the door in case the monks and *lamas* (priests) are in prayer. It is customary to leave a small donation of a few rupees at the altar and to ask before taking photographs, especially of divine images.

As the sun nears the horizon it is time to pedal the 8km (5 miles) home to Kathmandu. Head out the main entrance and turn right, pedalling westerly to a busy intersection. Turn left, go about ½km (¼ mile) past a small replica of the Bodhnath stupa, and take the next right. Stay on the paved road as it joins another; go right, descending to the bridge and up the other side. Turn right at the top, and follow this street all the way back to the Royal Palace in Kathmandu.

Blowing horns at Bodnath

Day 3

Patan to Panauti

Biking Distance: 51km (32 miles); Biking Time: 8–9 hours

Start in Patan, weaving your way through the maze of lanes with richly decorated woodcarved windows. Be dazzled by the ornate Golden Temple and wander through the incomparable Patan Durbar Square. Head southeast over the Valley rim to Panauti, venerable home of Nepal's oldest temple. A difficult off-road ride to Panauti with Himalayan views; then a paved road return to Kathmandu. Only fit and experienced bikers should undertake this tough ride.

Make your way to the **Bagmati River** which divides Kathmandu and Patan. Not long ago, rice paddies separated the two cities but today urban infill has replaced the rice with low rise buildings.

After crossing Patan Bridge, climb past the sleek Himalaya Hotel and turn left immediately past it. Stay on the main road and enter the ancient kingdom at **Patan Gate**. Follow the flow of traffic down the small main lane.

Wind your way down this narrow street until you come to **Kwa Bahal** (Golden Temple), well worth a walking tour. This splendid 15th-century monastery is your first introduction to the exquisite metalcraft for which Patan is renowned. The main temple, dedicated to Sakyamuni Buddha, is roofed with gilded copper with much of the façade covered with fine *repousse* work. The entrance is guarded by a pair of stone lions. All four corners of the compound have stone images dating from the 8th century.

Kwa Bahal entrance, Patan

From the main door, go right past curio shops and two small temples. Turn left and head straight into **Patan Durbar Square**. This spiritual heart of Patan is filled with handsome architectural monuments.

Patan Durbar Square

Roam briefly through it – by foot or by bike – for a long ride awaits today.

Facing south, to your left is **Mangal Hiti**, a water tank 4m (13ft) below ground. Excavated in the 10th-century Licchavi period, this bath is probably the oldest structure in the square. Three stone crocodile heads still pour out water.

Immediately on your right is Bhimsen, popular god of businessmen, who sits on the upper floor of his three-tiered home. A carved wooden panel on the south elevation narrates episodes from Bhimsen's life. Beyond stands **Krishna Mandir**, an impressive 17th-century stone temple of the *shikhara* style, with delicate relief carvings from the *Ramayana* and *Mahabharata* Hindu epics on the lower lintel band. Next, **Char Narayan** temple, all roof, door and window, invites visitors to sheltered circumambulation inside. The dominating **Hari Shanker Temple** at the south end of the square is guarded by appropriately robust kneeling elephants.

Extending down the length of the eastern side of the square is the **Patan Royal Palace** complex. It is made up of three *chowks* (courtyards), the palace buildings and two temples. The first *chowk* to your left, **Mani Keshab Narayan**, is occupied by a museum. The two temples, **Taleju and Degutaleju**, are accessible only to priests. Note the handsome metal doorway and the finely carved roof struts of **Mul Chowk**, next in line. The last courtyard to the south, **Sundari Chowk**, was designed as the residence of King Siddhi Narasingha Malla. At the centre is a beautiful bathing tank, its perimeter ringed by a pair of serpents and its walls covered with carvings of gods.

Leaving Sundari Chowk, turn left and exit the square by the southeast corner, diagonally opposite from where you entered it.

As you leave Patan, pause to appreciate the fact that this route is over 1,000 years old. Sacred stones along the way were worshipped before many of our home countries existed!

After a 5-minute ride, you reach the wide and busy Ring Road. Cross the road and head to the village of **Lubhu**, 5km (3 miles) beyond, just past a heavy concentration of wood and charcoal-fired brick factories. The clay soil here is suitable for brick-making.

Along the road you pass through picturesque Newari villages with houses contrasting beautifully against the backdrop of the snow-capped Himalayan range.

Reaching Lubhu in 20 minutes, you pass a small *dhara* (water spout) on your right. A statue of the three main gods of Hinduism presides over it. In the village you hear the clacking of the weaving machines that produce Nepali handloom cotton, Lubhu's main industry. The paved road picks up again just after the town square with a *pipal* tree and Shiva temple to the right.

On the way to Panauti

Thirty minutes beyond Lubhu you reach **Sisneri**, a quiet, classic middle hills village. The ethnicity of the people change as you get higher: Tamangs, Thakuris and Chhetris replacing the lowland Newari farmers. Life has a peaceful tempo here. Livestock roam in and out of ground floor rooms, elders sit and weave or tend to grandchildren while sons and daughters work the fields. At the village edge, the trail passes a large school in a clearing. Just beyond, the road makes a sharp left turn and begins one of the many switchbacks up to the saddle above. The ascent is 525m (1,600ft), steep and continuous with few level surfaces, but in good condition.

Stop along this grade for fantastic photo opportunities of yourself and friends biking out of the Kathmandu Valley with the Himalaya as backdrop. On a clear day it does not get any better than this! Watch for a special photo spot, 45 minutes out of Lubhu.

Fifteen minutes before the saddle there is a water source and chance to fill up your bottles (don't forget iodine to purify your drinking water) and a tea shop ahead. Get ready to see a school and remember that these kids are not used to seeing foreigners. They will be very curious, so be patient and do not lose your sense of humour. If you feel yourself getting hot under the collar, just ride off; they will not follow you far.

After your victorious arrival at the top, the descent is steep and steady, so hang on. At the trail junction take either way; both join up again shortly. The views are inviting but do not gaze long for you might ride off the trail and you are a long way from help.

At the second trail junction on this descent stay on the high trail to the right through Magar, Tamang and Chhetri homesteads. Before descending 300m (1,000ft) to **Manedobhan,** the trail seems to disappear where it crosses fields and two wooden bridges. It reforms as a dirt road and leads left into town where you can get food, tea and biscuits.

The route descends to a village along a meandering river where you may see planting, harvesting or house construction activities, depending upon the season.

The road is well-defined from Manedobhan to Panauti and needs no directions. As you get closer to Panauti, the villages become more urbanised, and the road visibly deteriorating from the heavy vehicles plying them. Stop and play *carom* with the kids if you see the gameboard set up along the road. It looks like checkers but is played more like billiards except that you flick the pieces across the chalky surface with your fingers.

Just before reaching Panauti you have spectacular views of the Himalaya again on your left. At the bus park, stop for a cold drink and change your pace before entering this ancient

Rambunctious children

city where the Buddha was a prince in a former lifetime.

Panauti, a classic Newari town, is off the beaten tourist trail and perhaps for this reason has received little attention for historic preservation, though it is now being restored by the French. Besides having a rich fabric of old streetscape, it is home to the oldest dated temple in Nepal, the Indreshwar Mahadev.

The town rests at the confluence of three rivers, one of which is

Fields framed by a rainbow near Panauti

invisible except to sages as the story goes. Panauti is believed to date from over 1,700 years ago and was, according to Nepali lore, a home of the Buddha in a past incarnation. Known as Prince Mahasattva, he offered his body to a starving tigress so that she and her cubs would not die. This act of supreme compassion is honoured at the nearby Buddhist pilgrimage site, Namo Buddha (see *Hike Itinerary 17*).

Biking the curves

To reach the temple complex from the bus park, cross the concrete bridge to the left bank of the stream. Re-cross at the suspension bridge. The 13th-century **Indreshwar Mahadev** temple is in a large courtyard to the right. The supporting struts of the temple roof are some of the earliest and finest examples of woodcarving in Nepal. Unlike most temple struts, these figures are carved from a single piece of wood, rendering a remarkably graceful form. In a later period, the arms were carved separately and fixed to the torso.

After visiting the temple, walk out the same door you entered and head straight toward the confluence of the two rivers. See if you can see the third! It is usually very peaceful here and a good spot for a discreet snack atop one of the temple plinths.

Bike back to the suspension bridge, turn left in front of it and wander back through town. From the bus park head out on the paved road, aiming for the white mountains if they are visible, following the many buses on their way to Kathmandu. If you are tired and cannot pedal another inch, you can negotiate with a minibus to take you and your bike for the trip back to Kathmandu. It will be at least the price for two persons, if not more.

Otherwise, take the paved road north to the Arniko Highway, turn left at the statue in the road at **Banepa** and ride about 2½ hours to Kathmandu. From Bhaktapur you can follow the electric trolley lines all the way back to Tripureshwor. Veer left at the roundabout, passing the stadium and GPO back to town.

Bikers attract interest in Sisneri

Right: afternoon tête-à-tête at Panauti

Bike-itineraries

1. Nagarjun

Distance: 42km (26 miles); Biking Time: 4–5 hours/half day

Climb nearly 700m (2,200ft) through dense forest to the sacred spot where the famous Buddhist philosopher Nagarjuna is said to have meditated, enjoying views of the Valley and Himals.

Besides being a pilgrimage to historic sites, this long steady climb offers a rigorous work-out. Bring plenty of water as there is none along the trail.

Start from the **Chetrapati 'bandstand'** in Kathmandu, and head

Prayer flags atop Nagarjun

north up this ancient lane. After a few minutes you reach Naya Bazaar, a bustling corner of town that brings out the worst in noisy engines with billowing clouds of exhaust; but hold on, it gets better.

Turn left, heading downhill (west). At the Ring Road roundabout, just 10 minutes away, cross and enter **Balaju**.

Continue uphill through the bazaar and straight at the T-junction, climbing slowly up the Nagarjun road. In just 10 minutes you will reach the main gate to the **Nagarjun Preserve** – the Queen's Forest – where you pay a 50 paisa entry fee.

The preserve, also known as Rani Ban, is one of a few protected forests within the Kathmandu Valley and is home to leopards, wild boars, foxes and many species of birds. Consider yourself lucky if you see them. Rhesus monkeys will, however, probably cross your path at some point. Do not touch or feed them – let them be and they will do likewise.

At the first fork in the road, go left and downhill. The road is moderately rocky and bumpy but the thick forest and shady canopy will seem to cushion your ride. The road winds southwesterly and you skirt behind Balaju Gardens with a good view of Swayambhunath to the left.

44

Bamboo-shaded descent

Ahead and to the south is Ichangu saddle which is said to be protected by Nagarjun. The route is gradual for about the first kilometre (½ mile). Just past the checkpost a rocky section signals the start of your climb to the top. On your right is a temple to Bhairav, marked with tridents. Behind the temple is a trail that leads to one of the sacred caves of Nagarjun.

Continue riding and after about 15 minutes you will break out of the forest and get a great view of Kathmandu. To the south is a *gompa* (monastery) perched atop Kimdol Hill, and the little valley that leads to Ichangu Narayan.

Approximately 2 hours from the start of your ride you will come to a grassy clearing on your left which forms a saddle. On the far side of the clearing is a trail that provides an alternative exit route after you return from the top.

Continue climbing on the road. It is steep and will require lots of effort and your lowest gear. It is another 30 minutes to the top and will be a push for some but well worth the effort.

At the summit is a *chorten* (Buddhist shrine) and an iron tower for even better views. The whole Valley is at your feet. Think of the travellers and pilgrims coming down from the high and arid desert plateau of Tibet. Imagine their spontaneous delight upon seeing this lush green valley.

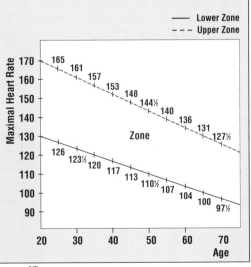

Average Condition Heart Rate Levels

Ideally, to improve aerobic conditioning, you should attempt to reach a heart rate within the zone and sustain it for a period of 20 minutes or longer, 3 times a week. If, during that period of time you are able to make the heart rate rise above the zone (eg. climbing a steep hill or riding faster), then the aerobic conditioning improves even more rapidly than with endurance exercises alone.

— Lower Zone
- - - Upper Zone

Maximal Heart Rate

Upper Zone values: 165, 161, 157, 153, 148, 144½, 140, 136, 131, 127½

Lower Zone values: 126, 123½, 120, 117, 113, 110½, 107, 104, 100, 97½

Zone

Age: 20, 30, 40, 50, 60, 70

Eager faces

After a good rest and perhaps a snack (this is a popular picnic spot for Nepalis and Tibetans on Saturdays), begin your descent. Take care not to go too fast; the road surface is *raato maato* (red clay-like mud) and very slippery when wet. It takes about 3 hours for a slow descent with stops for photos.

At the saddle just below the summit take the aforementioned turn-off to the right for my recommended and less travelled off-road route down. The forest is thicker and the road rougher. When you reach the main gate, turn right on the paved road back to Kathmandu.

2. Nage Gompa

Distance: 32km (20 miles); Biking time: 4 hours/half day

Ride straight north out of Kathmandu to Budhanilkantha village and the Reclining Vishnu. Climb up the steep slopes of Shivapuri to Nage Gompa. A straightforward strenuous ride with a cruise downhill if you return by the same route; or you can go on for a challenging off-road adventure, culminating at Bodhnath Stupa.

Leave Kathmandu and head north towards Budhanilkantha. Pass the beautiful Bansbari bamboo grove and drop down into the fertile fields of northern Kathmandu Valley. Just above the bus stop at Budhanilkantha, stop in to see the **Reclining Vishnu Temple** complex immediately on your left. It is walled in beyond a parking area.

This Reclining Vishnu dates from the 6th century when the area was the centre of the vanished Licchavi town of **Thatungri Dranga**. The massive image was carved from a 5-m (16-ft) long black stone that was dragged from elsewhere as the type of rock is unknown in the Valley.

Leave the Reclining Vishnu and snake slowly straight on north up the steep climb to the **Shivapuri Watershed and Wildlife Pre-**

The Reclining Vishnu

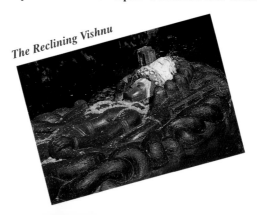

Trails are shared with villagers

serve. Just inside the gate is a big sign showing the preserve's road system. As you climb higher up the winding road, views of the Valley below and the surrounding mountains expand. The climb to **Nage Gompa** will take at least 1 hour from the gate. Fork right after the first switchback and at the third big curve, after the road has levelled out, you must keep an eye out for steps that cut into the hillside on your left. You will know you missed the trail if you turn the corner and see a small house bedecked with prayer flags in the distance.

As there is no place to safely lock your bike, carry and push it at least up to the nunnery. Walk up to the *gompa* (monastery) and enjoy the serenity of the setting. If perchance there is a *puja* (religious celebration) going on inside, you may be permitted to sit and watch it. Tulku Urgyen Rinpoche, renowned teacher and master of

Tibetan Buddhism, is the head *lama*. Often in retreat, he is not available to the general public.

After your visit to the *gompa*, retrace your steps back to the road where you have two options. You can simply return to Kathmandu the way you came or, if you are an experienced off-road rider and do not mind carrying and pushing for the sake of adventure, head down the slopes to Bodhnath.

Good sense and skill are required. Go another 5 minutes to the small house with the prayer flags from where you begin your descent south. The trail starts just before the house. If you lose the trail, just ask for **Bodhnath**.

Villagers may warn that you cannot ride these trails. They are not totally wrong. The first hour following the ridge is steep and tricky, requiring advanced skills. Even a professional would dismount and carry occasionally, so gauge your ability and be cautious.

After an hour the trail reaches a more rideable ridge and meanders through a beautiful pine forest. There are some tricky hair-pin turns and downhills, mostly rideable. On your right, looking to the west, are the fertile paddy fields surrounding Tupek and Tusal, the terrain of *Bike Itinerary 5*. You can also see Nagarjun mountain in the far distance, met in *Day 1*, and *Bike Itineraries 1* and *7*. To the northeast you will see the holy Bagmati River with Sankhu village and Nagarkot mountain in the far distance (*Bike Itinerary 8*).

An uphill climb

The trail then descends to a junction where you can either take the downhill road on your left or stay high on the ridge. The road to the left is direct and takes you to the saddle below. I always choose the high road because of the better view, riding partway down the steep slope and carrying for about 10 minutes to the saddle.

The left hand road descends to a saddle with a big *pipal* tree and tea shops just over the saddle. Follow the road for 10 to 15 minutes to another saddle and great Valley views. Look to your left – you cannot miss the dense dark green forest of **Gokarna**, home to Gokarna Safari Park (*Hike Itinerary 13*).

Going straight at the next junction will put you on the road to **Gokarna Mahadev Temple**, built on the banks of the Bagmati River in the 14th century. Each June on Gokarna Aunshi, or Father's Day, Hindu men who have lost an elder male in their household come to pray for departed souls. Magnificently carved wooden struts hold up the roofs of this three-tiered temple and the quality of the stone statues is testimony to the sensitive eyes and hands of the ancient Newari artisans.

Follow the road south and turn right at the T-junction which takes you on to Bodhnath. Stop for a snack at the **Stupa View Restaurant** before you return to Kathmandu.

3. Tokha

Distance: 18km (11 miles); Biking Time: 2 hours/half day

Directly north of Kathmandu is a short bike ride that encompasses the spectrum of downtown, suburban and rural Kathmandu. Your destination is Tokha, a typical ancient Valley village. An easy off-road jaunt.

Start out at the **Thamel-Kantipath** roundabout and head north for about 5km (3 miles) towards Budhanilkantha, crossing the Ring Road-Bansbari intersection. At **Hatigoda**, 2½km (1½ miles) from the Ring Road, turn west (left) onto a straight dirt track just beyond a string of shops. If you have difficulty finding the turning, ask anyone for the main route to **Tokha**.

Tokha terrain

The road is wide, starting with a gentle climb through small villages. Turn right at both of the first two Y-junctions and go downhill. Many of the people living here commute daily to work in Kathmandu. They might live in mud and straw-walled farmhouses but emerge each morning in white shirts for their jobs in five-star hotels.

Head west and downhill to the sacred **Vishnumati River**. The trail passes through idyllic pockets of rice paddy and bamboo groves. To the north you may see Shivapuri mountain and in the foreground, the fertile terraces that step up to Budhanilkantha (see *Bike Itinerary 2* and *Hike Itinerary 18*).

A Newari facade

You must ford the Vishnumati River, but even at the height of the monsoon, it is only about 30cm (1ft) deep. Don't worry, mountain bikes are made to ride right through a little challenge like this. As there is no bridge, you have no choice but to get your feet wet. Make sure you are in the right gear to make the crossing. In both front and rear wheels your chain should be in the middle chain ring. Get a headstart, entering the river with some momentum, and pedal hard and fast. Do not worry about your pedals being under the water – you can go right through this with no sweat.

Riding through rice fields

Take the trail on your right, riding through fields on paddy bunds (low ridges that separate one paddy field from another). Turn right at the next T-junction and again follow the trail (not the steps) to the right for 2–3 minutes up to **Tokha**. You will arrive at a lively town square where you can buy biscuits and fill your water bottles. Do not drink the tap water without treating it first with iodine. Go see the two-tiered temple of **Bhimsen** (a deity worshipped for his strength and courage) just beyond the square. At the doorway or just inside many shops you will see photographs of this popular god.

Go back to the square, turn right and enter Tokha proper where children may be yelling *'Namaste'*, 'bye-bye' and generally being rambunctious. Elders peer down from their simple carved windows; buffalo gaze out from ground floor stables and you may feel that the Middle Ages is still alive.

Just outside Tokha, take the dirt path right to a **Kali Temple** and the village cremation grounds. Kali is a female aspect of Shiva, and is both giver and taker of life. She can be recognised by the skulls she wears. The villagers have often warned me to be careful around the temple, not to anger Kali lest harm might come to me.

If you have come during kite season, September–October, the field may be filled with children flying kites.

Tokha

Continue past the Kali temple on the well-worn path, staying high on the plateau and turning left at the next Y-intersection. You are heading towards **Baniyatar**, a large Brahman Chhetri village.

To your right and left you will see low lying valleys traditionally used for cultivation but now being consumed for housing Kathmandu's ever-increasing population.

Just south of the village is a large *pipal* tree where the route descends through a sandy stretch to the valley floor below. Cross over the Vishnumati, by bridge this time, and follow the road to **Gogabu**.

Bathing beauty

Take a left turn at the T-junction inside Gogabu and your next intersection will be Ring Road. Go straight across and continue into Kathmandu. The road ends at a busy T-junction.

Turn left, passing the **Malla Hotel** on the right. Its spacious garden is ideal for a cold drink and a rest. Turn right at the next intersection and you will reach the Thamel roundabout.

4. Ichangu Narayan

Distance: 23km (14 miles); Biking Time: 3 hours/half day

Ride west out of town along the ancient route to the Buddhist stupa, Swayambhunath. Spin the enormous prayer wheels for the betterment of mankind and join the pilgrims circumambulating the stupa. Pass through Swayambhunath village, cross Ring Road and head for the quiet village of Ichangu, home to one of the four most important Vishnu temples in the Valley. A gentle, dirt road ride.

This short excursion starts in **Thamel** or **Chetrapati** and follows the same path out to **Swayambhunath** and Ring Road as *Day 1*.

The road running west past the **Ani Gompa** (Tibetan Buddhist Nunnery) will take you gradually up and out of the Valley. **Ring Road**, completed in 1976, was expected to be the boundary of development for a long time, but already farmers are surrendering more and more land for residential use. The traditional export of food from Kathmandu Valley to India has now been reversed.

Do not forget to turn around to see the Swayambhunath *stupa* silhouetted against the townscape of Kathmandu. At the next intersection take the road going up, past a rock quarry. At the saddle is a temple of **Halchowk Bhairav** and a good place for a tea stop and photo shoot. You can ask the vendor to watch your bike

as you walk up the steps to Halchowk, the little village above, for a great view back.

Retrace your steps down and ride on for about 15 minutes to **Ichangu**, a small village with the Vishnu temple complex of **Ichangu Narayan** at the end of the road. The main temple lost its primary deity to thieves so you may find the inhabitants ambivalent about showing the others.

This temple is one of the four most holy Narayan (Vishnu) temples in Nepal. During the Haribodhini Ekadasi festival in October–November an all-day pilgrimage links the four complexes of Changu Narayan, Bishankhu Narayan, Sekh Narayan and Ichangu Narayan.

Return the same route and stop for lunch at the **Hotel Vajra**, or if you feel like some good

Early morning mists in winter

ol' meat and potatoes, continue on into Thamel and head for the **Old Vienna Inn**, located within the Gourmet delicatessen.

5. Gomcha

Distance: 26km (16 miles); Biking Time: 2½–3 hours/half day

Not exactly a harrowing Indiana Jones adventure, this short and exciting ride takes you through the outbacks north of Ring Road. You will pass ancient villages and acres of terraced rice fields – a testimony to Newari farming skills – as you head to the temple of Kali. An off-road rowdy romp.

Go to the Bansbari-Ring Road intersection and head east towards Bodhnath. Just past the bridge that spans the **Dhobi Khola** river, turn left onto a dirt road, and drop down to the river. Stay to its right, heading due north. Follow this undulating road through the village of **Mahankal**. Most of these homes house people working in the carpet industry: weavers, spinners and the shopkeepers who serve them. Carpet making is a very important industry in Nepal, employing thousands of workers, mostly women from the hills.

The road is wide but rutted. On a clear day, **Ganesh Himal**, at 7,111m (21,890ft) can be seen to your left at 11 o'clock and **Kopan Monastery** atop the hill directly in front of you. Turn right at the T-junction after about 10–15 minutes and go uphill. Turn left before the top, in front of the shops. The road, again heading north, narrows to a walking trail and eventually comes to a T-intersection with a wide dirt road. Turn left and go up the hill.

The village sprawl you are passing through is using valuable agricultural land but, as this residential expansion has created new roads into scenic territory, we may as well use them. At the next Y-turning, take the left road which drops down and then climbs a short but steep section curving left with pleasant views looking

Gomcha's Vajra Kali

Sacred pipal tree overwhelms a shrine

back on your trail. As the road levels off, you reach an intersection with a white *mandir* (temple) on your left. Turn left and go up the hill. If you are going to Kopan take the right fork of the next Y-junction and go uphill, reaching it in about 5 minutes.

There are beautiful views to your left of the Valley below and the populated ridges to the west. At the next Y-intersection stay on the high trail to the right of the *pipal* tree. The road will descend to the valley behind Kopan Monastery. The road is badly rutted and you have to be skilful to ride down, so walk where you must.

As you descend, you will notice pockets of fertile fields sculpted into the Valley walls, dominated by Shivapuri mountain just beyond. You may see farmers tending their fields or whole villages planting seedlings before monsoon or harvesting in the autumn. Ride down to the Valley floor, cross a small stream and climb steeply up toward **Tupek**, a Newari village noted for its mud house builders. As you ascend, take the left hand fork up a steep furrowed section to enter the village from the north.

You will pass through the seemingly forgotten medieval village of Tupek, dominated by a large mud-hole in which water buffalo wallow in during the monsoon. Drop down to your left out of Tupek and turn right at the next Y-junction heading toward **Tusal**. At the entry of the village the road turns left and skirts the main village. Up and to your right from this junction is a small *mandir* which houses a beautiful 1.2-m (4-ft) stone sculpture of **Karunamaya**, an emanation of Avalokiteshwara. You should be aware that ancient images like these are being stolen for export and thus many villagers fear foreigners showing interest or taking photos of them. Be sensitive and if they show disapproval, do not take photographs.

Continue around the village and through the school yard beyond Tusal heading for **Gomcha**. The road is level and you are high on a ridge looking down at terraced riverside rice paddies. The gorge gets narrower as you approach Gomcha and the **Kali Temple** which sits on the steep Dhobi Khola banks. Arrive at Gomcha, entering a big sloping field to the west of the village. The temple is down by the stream. Even fearsome Kali's environs has a rest spot for the faithful; have a lunch break under the shade of the big *pipal* tree.

Kali, the female Hindu form of destruction, is deeply revered and feared in Nepal. To appease Kali, blood must be offered by animal sacrifices at her temples.

Village scene

Below and just to the north of the temple is an old foot bridge with a stone statue of **Tangton Gyalpo**, the great 15th-century Tibetan builder who is said to have built the first iron bridges in Tibet. This is the only known image of this ancient engineer in Kathmandu Valley. Was this bridge built in the 15th century? Archaeologists and scholars will have to figure that out but I'm content to believe that the venerable Tibetan wandered down to Nepal for a holiday and could not stop himself from doing what he did best.

Your trail runs south, to the left of the *pipal* tree. You can see it continuing up the other side of the river. Prepare for a river crossing by getting in the right gear and pedalling hard to the other side. Or, you could carry your bike across the bridge if you want to avoid getting your feet wet.

After a steep climb, the westward path opens up to fertile paddy fields. Depending upon the season, you may be riding through an undulating sea of rice or wheat for approximately 30 minutes before you reach the paved road.

Your ride ends with one last descent and a steep short climb before you meet the paved Budhanilkantha Road. Turn left and ride to Kathmandu in about 20 minutes. Quench your thirst and appetite tonight at the **Bhancha Ghar** restaurant (Tel: 225172), which serves Nepalese food in an authentic old Newari home.

Stone sculpture of Karunamaya at Tusal

6. Bungamati

Distance: 41km (25 miles); Biking Time: 5–6 hours/full day

Ride south to the villages of Bungamati and Khokana where ancient rituals still capture the hearts of the inhabitants. Follow a forested climb to the village of Champi overlooking the southwestern corner of the Valley. Vajra Varahi and Tika Bhairav are must-see's in this temple-studded town. A combination of downhill push and uphill carry are required for this romp through rough terrain to Chapagaon, Lele and back to Kathmandu.

Check your maps for **Jawalakhel**, south of Kathmandu and Patan. Look for the **Zoo** and the **Tibetan Refugee Centre**, each worth a visit, one for its Himalayan wildlife and the other for its stunning Tibetan carpets. If you do not find the carpet you want here, come back another day and check out any of the shops in the area. Continue on to Ring Road and cross it heading south on a dirt road.

Few visitors wander this far from the Durbar Squares. Plan to take time and absorb life in these quiet villages, far from modern amenities and the ever-faster life of downtown Kathmandu.

Go downhill, passing a small temple on your right. Enter **Naku Village**, taking the left fork over the metal bridge, and then left again uphill at the paved road. Continue past *pipal* trees on your left and right – good vantage spots for scenic views. From just beyond the tree on the western (right) side, you can see Bungamati on the left and Khokana on the right. Notice how tightly compacted these traditional farming settlements are, maximising agricultural land. No wonder everyone in town knows each other.

Look across at the hill of Champa Devi and the Bagmati River below where it flows through Chobar Gorge on its way out of the Valley. Follow the road towards **Bungamati**, and after the first building go down a steep rocky section to your right. At the next

A balancing act with Bungamati in the distance

Harvest time at Khokana

intersection, the flagstone paving goes straight but you go right on a dirt path. Pass through a courtyard, exiting right.

The trail is rocky and takes you through rice fields. It is difficult to pedal, so walk where you need to. The trail will descend again, this time into **Khokana**. Take the left fork into town and turn at the first road on your right. Stop at the temple of **Shekali Mai**, or Rudrayani, a Valley nature goddess. A bit farther on your right is a beautiful statue of Lakshmi, goddess of wealth and prosperity, housed in a small *dharmasala* (rest house for pilgrims).

As an option for experts bikers only, continue straight for an off-road adventure, down across the Bagmati and up the other side to return via Chobar Gorge. After crossing the river, the trail turns right, gradually ascending to the paved Dakshinkali road. Follow the road to **Chobar Gorge**, just past the cement factory and visit **Binayak Ganesh Temple** there. Follow the trail over the bridge to the east side of the river, wind up and northward, meeting the road on which you began this ride, taking you to Ring Road. You know the way from here.

Elephant-headed Ganesh

Otherwise, return from Khokana to Bungamati. Five minutes before re-entering the village is a forested knoll to your right, home to **Karya Binayak**, or Ganesh the elephant-headed God. Behind his temple, take in the serene view of farmhouses nestled among rice fields. Looking southwest you can see Pharping, a community of Buddhist monasteries and retreat centres (see *Hike Itinerary 16*).

Spinning wool for the Valley's huge carpet industry

Return to the trail, turn right and follow the flagstone path into Bungamati. You may see women at their daily tasks; spinning wool, tending babies or picking lice out of *bahini's* (little sister's) hair. The trail will take you to a gate guarded by two large lions, entrance to the main temple of **Rato Machhendranath**.

Just beyond the far end of the square you may notice a pit on your right. Here, once every 12 years, the Chariot of Rato Machhendranath is assembled. A 7½-m (25-ft) tall tower of bamboo is lashed with twine to a wooden chassis with 2-m (6-ft) diameter wooden wheels. The men from Bungamati must drag the image of Rato Machhendranath in this ungainly chariot all the way to Patan – a task which can take many weeks. The success or failure of the massive communal undertaking is believed to foretell the villages' fortune for the next 12 years. Thousands of onlookers come to enjoy the wild excitement of the chariot's voyage and to receive *dharshan*, or blessings, by witnessing it.

The road loops through the main bazaar of Bungamati and uphill out of town. If you are tired take your bike and hop onto the bus back to Kathmandu. When you reach the outskirts of Bungamati you will have made a complete loop and ended up where you turned off to go down to Khokana.

The road continues to the right up a steep hill passing a large *pipal* tree. Follow this road to **Cunikhel**. To the east is the ridge on which you will return.

A series of short hills takes you through Chhetri villages surrounded with thick

The author contemplating the Rato Machhendranath chariot

forest. Just after Cunikhel the road splits. Go to the left towards a big *pipal* tree at the top of the hill. At a small temple, go down to your left just before the road ends at **Champi**. Continue to your left to a field with a big *pipal* tree at the far end. To the left of the tree a trail descends steeply. Get off and push your bike if you are not an experienced downhill rider (3 minutes).

At the next *pipal* tree the trail turns to steep steps. Use the push-bike technique for about 5 minutes from here to the river. Look up to your right at the road that takes you to the village of Lele on the other side of the mountain, your option from Chapagaon.

Chapagaon-Lele Valley

Cross the river at the bamboo bridge and keep your eyes open for egrets. To reach **Chapagaon** village you must carry your bike up the steps (15–20 minutes). Or, you can wait until someone passes who looks interested in making a few rupees by carrying your bike. You might pay them about Rs 10 for this. After the steps you will reach Chapagaon in another 5–10 minutes.

Turn right at the paved road heading south out of Chapagaon. Turn right again the next intersection and climb up to the right of Bhaga Ban village. The road gives you commanding views of the distant Bagmati River and of the Nakhu Khola immediately down to your right.

Continue on, looking down to your right just before you reach the other side of the mountain. You will notice a huge *sal* tree and a large brick wall covered by a tin roof at the confluence of the two rivers. The temple of **Tika Bhairav** is here, housed in a simple shelter and can easily be bypassed. Ride down to see the abstract

Bungamati community effort

Strings of red chilies drying in Chapagaon

polychrome mural (3m x 6m/10ft x 20ft) of Bhairav's face painted on the inside wall. He is worshipped in the form of a large boulder with a small altar for sacrificial offerings.

Continue on the main road reaching **Anandaban** (peaceful forest) and the home of the **Leprosy Hospital**. Five minutes beyond the turn-off for the hospital main gate, look for the sign to **Lele Memorial Park** built by Pakistan International Airlines. Lock your bike to the bike rack or tree and walk up for a short visit. Return to your bike and continue on to the sleepy village of **Lele**. Turn left in the middle of town and head up to the saddle where you get views of the valley below. Follow the road back to Chapagaon.

Go straight through Chapagaon. At the Krishna sculpture on your right is a dirt road that leads to the forested **Vajra Varahi Temple** (10 minutes), an important Astha Matrika (Eight Mother Goddesses) shrine.

To return on the main Chapagaon road from Vajra Varahi, retrace your route to the Krishna sculpture and turn right. Three minutes further, note the two sadly neglected temples with beautiful woodcarvings of Krishna and Narayan. At the far side of town you will pass a trio of images – Ganesh, Brahma and a large *yoni*. The *yoni* is a female fertility form worshipped throughout the Valley. Ganesh is the popular elephant-headed Hindu god of wisdom and remover of obstacles.

Just past Chapagaon is **Thecho**, a charming village marked with a peacock set atop a stone pillar in front of **Balkumari Temple**.

Surrounding this temple are several *paathis*, stone seats where you can sit and watch the life of the village. To the north is a temple to **Brahmayani** with her vehicle, the swan, atop a stone column guarded by lions.

The last village of the day is **Sunakothi**, the 16th-century home of the **Bringareshwar Mahadev Temple**, which houses the Valley's 64 most sacred *linga*, the phallic symbol for Shiva. Some towns are known for their good chillies, some for their soccer team. Others have armies of phalluses – a formidable foe if you happen to be rooting for family planning.

Bringareshwar Mahadev Temple

When you reach Ring Road, turn left and take the next right up the paved road to retrace your path into Kathmandu. If hunger prevents you from making it any farther, grab a piece of cake or a sandwich at **Woody's German Bakery**, just beyond the Jawalakhel roundabout. For something more substantial, stop in at the **Hotel Himalaya**, halfway down the hill on your right.

7. Kakani

Distance: 45km (28 miles); Biking Time: 6–8 hours/1–2 days

Climb 702m (2,300ft) to Kakani. Spend the night at the modest Taragaon Hotel and rise the next day for an off-road adventure around Ahale Dara on the Valley's northwest rim. Descend to Budhanilkantha.

Remember to take plenty of water and food for this long ride through steep and rough terrain. Pick up the route from *Day 1* and

'Gear Wallahs' at Kakani

Seeking local knowledge

continue up the road from **Teenpipli**, climbing the three shoulders of **Ahale Dara** to Kakani. The road mounts steadily with panoramic views down terraced hillside to the valley below. This ride along the south face can be hot and sweaty on a sunny day but the scenic views when you crest the ridge and meet the white peaks spread across the horizon are worth it. Turn right and continue up the paved road to Kakani.

This last section of the climb is the hardest but remember that it is not long so give it your best. At the top of the climb the road enters the small village of **Kakani** and makes a sharp left turn to the government-run **Taragaon Hotel**.

Spend the night and be treated to the dazzling array of colours as the sun sets on breathtaking Ganesh Himal, Langtang Lirung and Dorje Lakpa mountains. Awaken with the sun and catch more of the same in reverse. Have a hearty omelette and toast while you try to pick out the peaks and then head out for the day's adventure.

Across from the hotel is the evocative 19th-century Raj-style bungalow which has belonged to the British envoys since the mid-19th century and once marked the furthest point foreigners were allowed to venture outside the Kathmandu Valley.

Try your bumpy ride skills by riding down the long and shallow hotel steps. Turn left on the dirt road. After 4 minutes take the first left turn for a short visit to the **Kakani Memorial Park**. Lock your bike, climb the brick steps, pass through the entrance and visit the hilltop memorial to those who died in the plane crash of July 1992.

Retrace your steps, get on your bike and turn left back at the dirt road, heading on to the nursery farm gate. Take the trail to the right of the gate and push or carry your bike off-road for 30 minutes. You will reach a washout where you can see the road above you. Carry the bike up to the road.

Turn right towards the Valley. Your route was once a wide road but nature has reclaimed and refined it down to a single track. This ride is mostly downhill but do not be fooled: there are some difficult uphill climbs and places where you must dismount and carry, fortunately nothing more than a few minutes.

After passing the military camp you reach a saddle demarcating the half-way point of the ride, signalling greatly improved road conditions and a return to mountain views. Be careful on the next

Taking a break on the route east of Kakani

Having a splash

section of the road because it is travelled by cars and people carrying loads whom you could meet head-on in the middle of a turn!

At the saddle, turn right to return on the Kathmandu side of the mountain. The left turn road circles partway around Shivapuri mountain but to date is not completed. The road is interrupted by a deep and dangerous 150-m (500-ft) ravine where falling would be fatal. Do not go off-road!

The road to the right contours around the mountain, gradually descending to the **Tokha Military Hospital**. Just above the hospital a road comes in on your left. It is identifiable by a white *stupa* on the right amongst houses and the beginning of a steep descent.

Turn left and climb the short hill through a pine forest above the hospital. You will reach a waterfall where during the hot months you can hop into its refreshing waters to cool down and dry off as you ride.

The road is all downhill from here, descending to **Budhanilkantha** from the north. Look for Nage Gompa on the ridge to the east (see *Bike Itinerary 2* and *Hike Itinerary 18*).

At the only road intersection turn right, pass the large Shivapuri Watershed map on your right and exit through the gate. Ride cautiously downhill, remembering that the local people are not accustomed to seeing bicycles. If you have a bell, use it liberally to warn people in your path.

Pass Budhanilkantha and continue straight back to Kathmandu. From Budhanilkantha you can either bike all the way to Kathmandu, or if you prefer, take a public bus, minibus or taxi back.

Generations of labour have contoured the Valley

Distance: 76km (47 miles); Biking Time: 4 hours/1–2 days

An overnight in Nagarkot is your best bet for mountain views and a possible glimpse of Everest. I sometimes make this a full-moon night ride but if it is your first time, do it by day. Follow the old road through Thimi where potters throw pots and mask makers work with colourful papier-mâché. Climb to the Valley rim at Nagarkot where you can catch a Himalayan sunset and sunrise from the Vajra Farmhouse. After a leisurely morning ride down the back way, stop in Sankhu at the Bajra Jogini Temple, a monument to the Tantric form of Kali. Finish the ride at the great stupa of Bodhnath before heading back to Kathmandu.

Call the **Hotel Vajra** (Tel: 271545) and make reservations in advance for an overnight stay at the **Vajra Farmhouse**. One night's tariff of US$30 includes breakfast, lunch and dinner in a double room with shared facilities; US$40 buys you an attached bath. This lovely, simple lodge is isolated from the rest of the hotels on the northern side of Nagarkot with 180-degree views of the Himalaya. If you prefer the company of other tourists, I recommend the **Hotel Viewpoint** at the top of the mountain, a clean hotel with good food and a great view.

Himalaya from Nagarkot

Heading south down Durbar Marg, turn left at the King Mahendra statue. After passing the Royal Nepal Arts Academy on your right, turn left at the T-junction and right at the next junction. Immediately on your left is **Krishna Loaf Bakery**, home to Nepal's first machine-made bread. Stop in and grab a few confectionery goodies for the road. You can never eat too much while biking! Twenty years ago when I first came to Nepal, the bakery had just a modest sign saying 'Machine-made Bread' which seemed to me an odd thing to celebrate. But thinking back to childhood days I have a faint memory of comparing new and impressive things to 'sliced bread'. Nepal has come a long way since then.

Continue straight, heading due east past a busy intersection un-

Not mountain biking

til the road jogs left, straightens out and heads downhill. Cross the Dhobi Khola river and climb to **Gosala**, the Pashupatinath intersection on Ring Road. Cross over and continue towards the airport, pausing at the Bagmati River to see the roofs of **Pashupatinath**, the most important Hindu temple in the Valley (see *Day 2*).

Beyond the bridge the road climbs slightly as you pass the **Royal Nepal Golf Club** (Tel: 472836) on the left. Green fees of Rs 585 include clubs, three balls and tees plus a refundable Rs 500 deposit for the clubs.

Continuing along Ring Road, crest at the airport and go straight at the next roundabout (Old Baneswar) down a steep hill keeping left and up the next hill to the Koteswar roundabout. Turn left following the trolley wires and take your first left at the bottom of the hill. You are now on the old road to Bhaktapur. It will take you through Thimi, a quaint potters' and mask-makers' village.

The road to Bhaktapur is bordered by the well-kept and thriving vegetable farms belonging to the Newar *jyapu* (farmer) caste. On your left before Thimi you will pass the **Swiss SOS Children's Village**, an orphanage worth a visit.

You know that you have hit **Thimi** when clay lions, demons and bears leap out from all sides. This dedication to make-believe has swept the whole village, but my favourite shop is on the outskirts of Thimi, on the Bhaktapur side. The proprietors have a big supply of masks and do not mind showing you their workshop out back, a nice photo opportunity. Along the road you will see more potters throwing pots and crafting statues of guardians, elephants and rhinos from the unique black clay

of the area. Though attractive, getting the statues home is an ordeal because they are not glazed and are therefore especially delicate. Then again, the art is charming and inexpensive so it is worth a try.

Leaving Thimi the road sweeps right; in the distance, on the left, is a forested hillock. Just after a small bridge and before the hillock make a left turn onto a narrow paved road which will take you all the way to Nagarkot.

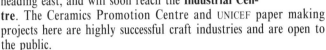

Patchwork fields

You are skirting the north side of **Bhaktapur**, heading east, and will soon reach the **Industrial Centre**. The Ceramics Promotion Centre and UNICEF paper making projects here are highly successful craft industries and are open to the public.

Soon you pass two roads on your left. The second takes you to the **Changu Narayan Village** and **Changu Narayan Temple** (see *Day 2*) atop a ridge that comes down from Nagarkot. The temple holds some of Nepal's oldest stone sculptures.

Here, in the outskirts of Bhaktapur, life spills into the streets. Garlands of chillies and garlic are draped to dry on red brick façades. Mothers and babies luxuriate in the sun with oil massages and animals are always on the wander.

Behind Bhaktapur, a stretch of flat road meanders through idyllic rural life, overlooking a textured carpet of rice paddy fields studded with bamboo groves and farmhouses. You and the occasional vehicle – tractor or rotor-tiller – are the only modernities in an ancient agricultural setting. As you start up the switchbacks, you can see the road behind you slithering across the Kathmandu Valley like a silver snake.

Where the road meets a dip in the ridge, a dirt track runs left. This is an alternate route to the temple complex of Changu Narayan. From this saddle you can see across the Valley floor to the village of Sankhu, with great views of the Himalayan range. The trail you will descend tomorrow contours the hillside to the northeast. About 10 minutes along the Nagarkot road you reach a pine forest, a rare experience in the Valley.

View from Nagarkot

Gateway to Sankhu

The road to **Nagarkot**, shared with the military, is not heavily travelled (except on Saturdays) but enough so that it is pitted and in disrepair. After climbing 590m (1,800ft) you arrive at **Lamatole**, distinguished by a large *pipal* tree, a small white *stupa* and tea stalls. Approximately 30 minutes beyond Lamatole you will reach a point on the ridge with views of both Kathmandu and Nagarkot. You can also see tomorrow's route and the start of the popular Helambu trekking trail.

The road traverses below the Nagarkot ridge; up ahead on your left you can see a little bazaar. Beyond this collection of tea stalls and shops the paved road curves right but you go left on a dirt road marked by lodge signs. Follow the road up a steep forested hill, passing the many rest houses. Walk if you are tired, you deserve to. Notice on your right the sign for **Hotel Viewpoint**, should you choose to stay here, or continue on over the summit.

Cresting the hill and completing your 713-m (2,340-ft) ascent, ride a few minutes down and stop at the sharp left hand turn to feast your eyes on a beautiful mountain panorama. From here you can see the **Vajra Farmhouse**, 15 minutes further along, with its hot showers and cold drinks for the weary. If you still have energy in reserve, hang out here for the sunset and complete the ride at dusk.

Village festival at Sankhu

After an early morning sunrise, I recommend a leisurely breakfast in the serenity of your hilltop perch. A departure as late as noon will still get you into Kathmandu before dark.

From the Farmhouse you can see your route below, with a fork just after a flat section. This is the last chance to see high mountains before you drop down to **Sankhu**. Take the left fork and continue traversing down the mountain. The right fork begins the trek to Shivapuri (*Hike Itinerary 20*).

The road condition changes from season to season and although quite wide, it gets rutted and washed out in some places. Carry your bike over the washouts and expect that unless you are accustomed to downhill riding, you will give your hands and brakes a heavy work-out.

As there are no side roads,

there is no way to get lost. Follow the dirt road and just before Sankhu you will cross a bridge and climb a short rise. Where the road turns right, go straight to the temple complex next to the river. Search out the *pipal* tree with an image of Vishnu embedded into the base of it. Here, people of the Valley gather to bathe in the chilly stream during the Magha Sankranti festival in January, marking the end of the cold season.

Enter Sankhu and make your way north, to the right side as you enter the town. Ask anyone to point the way to **Bajra Jogini** (a Tantric goddess) temple, following the wide path paved with stones, past beautiful sculptures and shrines to the stone steps. Lock your bike here to the metal poles or a tree.

The 10-minute climb to the temple complex is lined with old water tanks, rest houses and a vermillion-powder-and-blood-adorned triangular stone where animal sacrifices are made to the goddess. The temple has three gilded roofs and a fine golden *torana* over the main entrance with Bajra Jogini as centrepiece. It is believed that she was the motivating force behind Manjushri who drained the lake that once filled Kathmandu Valley.

Bajra Jogini Temple

Leaving the temple complex and Sankhu, you will travel on a paved road to Kathmandu, passing through gentle countryside and roadside villages. Pass Gokarna Safari Park on your right before reaching **Bodhnath**. Continue to the first major intersection, go left then right at the first street on your right. Follow the road down, across the Dhobi Khola river and up the other side where you will turn right and continue into downtown Kathmandu.

That was quite a work-out! If you are feeling achy, try a sauna at the Vajra or one of the major hotels' health clubs. Or how about a session of *hatha yoga* and a massage to unwind your sore muscles at **The Yoga House** (Tel: 416998). After that, if you feel like some good Indian food, try the **Ghar-e-Kabab**, on Durbar Marg (Tel: 221711 for reservations).

9. Dhunche to Gosainkund

Biking Distance: 105km (65 miles); Biking Time: 14–16 hours/4–6 days

This ride takes you over dirt roads to Dhunche where you can lock up and trek to the holy lakes in the Langtang Himal and back in four days. Alternatively, bike on for another day to the road's end.

Climb up and out of the Valley at Kakani (see *Bike Itinerary7*) and descend 1,355m (4,450ft) to the Tadhi Khola river. Mountain views keep you company and the condition of the road keeps your descent to a reasonable pace. At Trisuli Bazaar leave the paved road and start your off-road ride to **Dhunche**. The road climbs and

Sacred lake at Gosainkund

drops, hugging the Trisuli River, reaching Betrawati by the end of the first long day. Stay at the first lodge you see north of the Phalangu Khola.

The second day demands serious climbing up 1,375m (4,510ft) over a rock-strewn road to destination **Dhunche** at 2,000m (6,560ft). You have to pay a Rs 650 fee to enter the **Langtang National Park** and will also need a trekking permit. Be sure to get one before leaving Kathmandu.

From here you can hike up to **Gosainkund Lake (**4,590m/ 15,060ft) and back in four days, camping or staying in tea houses as you go. Beware of altitude sickness with elevation gain; spend two nights at **Sing Gompa** (3,250m/10,663ft) on the way up for proper acclimatization. It will be wise to use a trekking agency to take care of the trekking itinerary.

Legend says that Lord Shiva drank the world's poisons and went to Lake Gosainkund in the Himalaya to purify himself with glacier water. During the great Shiva festival of Janai Purnima (mid-July to mid-August), legend has it that a pious pilgrim will see the image of Shiva reflected on the lake's surface. Expect freezing temperatures at night and possibly snow on the ground from December through February.

Another alternative is to ride from Dhunche to the road's end at **Somdang** and return to **Syabrubensi** village for the night. Look

forward to a great downhill to Betrawati and then a last day's long climb back into the Kathmandu Valley powered by visions of filet mignon and baked alaska at the **Chimney Room** of the Hotel Yak and Yeti (Tel: 411436).

Syabrubensi village in Langtang National Park

10. Daman

Distance: 80km (50 miles); Biking Time: 8–10 hours/2 days

Leave the Valley at Thankot and negotiate a bumpy steep descent (762m/2,500ft) with expansive hill and Himal views. For skilled downhill riders the thrills are worth sharing the road with trucks. At the bottom, depart the highways and balance your day with a long quiet haul up through forested hills to the contemplative heights of Daman. A very strong rider can make it to Daman and back in a 10-hour day, but most of us will be happier with a night at the Everest Panorama Resort.

Ride to Thankot past the southwest Valley rim and descend 522m (1,500ft) on a paved road to **Naubise** where the road splits. One fork climbs up the **Tribhuvan Raj Path** (King's Way) and the other winds through Mugling to Pokhara, both ending up in the Terai lowlands. The Raj Path was the first road into Kathmandu Valley, built in 1953, and was the only route connecting with India until the Prithvi Raj Marg to Pokhara was completed in 1973.

Take the Raj Path which mounts steadily through oak and *chilaune* forests, passing several villages to 1,981m (6,500ft) where you begin your descent. From here it drops into the picturesque, extensively terraced **Palung Valley**, at its best abloom with yellow mustard. **Daman** (2,400m/7,874ft), last outpost before rolling down to the Terai lowlands, is unexpectedly inhabited by Sherpas (mountain people who more usually live near Everest or Helambu) who provide food and lodging for tourists and truckers. I recommend staying at the **Everest Panorama Resort** (Tel: 415372). Book in advance and they will come to Daman to whisk you away 3 km (1¾ miles) further up to their romantic hideaway. With 400km (250 miles) of panoramic snow-peak views, rock-climbing and local treks, this new resort is worth an extra day or two.

The Daman road winds through Nepal's middle hills

Rhododendrons are Nepal's national flower

The next day, visit the **Bhutanese monastery** in the quiet rhododendron-pine forest. Walk the 2km (1¼ mile) down the road to Daman and watch for a sign-posted trail off to the left. Hike the trail to the monastery for a brief visit. Return to your bike at the resort and ride the last 152m (500ft) to the top of Daman Pass and get ready for the ride of a life-time; snaking down 2,100m (6,900ft) through forests brilliant with rhododendron flowers in early spring and orchids in summer.

Speed demons beware. This downhill is a dream come true with no speed limits except your own bike handling skills and the awareness that traffic conventions are at best randomly followed by the Nepalis. Expect vehicles to pass on the inside of blind curves.

If you have carefully aimed to hit **Hetauda** in the autumn you can stop at the **Motel Avocado** (Tel: 057-20235/20429) for the delectable diversion of avocado omelettes and sandwiches, the only place in all of Nepal that serves such delicacies. It is also the only good hotel in Hetauda.

From here it is a perfectly flat highway ride to **Royal Chitwan National Park**. Arrange ahead of time if you plan to stay at one of the safari lodges, with the better ones located inside the park and budget variety set just outside at **Saurah**. From Hetauda, ride west to **Tadi Bazaar**, where you turn off the Terai's East-West Highway towards the park. Here you slip into timelessness, following handsome Tharu farmers, huge white oxen and wooden-wheeled carts.

Follow the road back to Kathmandu reversing your route, or arrange for transport on a bus or truck in Tadi Bazaar or Hetauda.

11. Kodari

Distance: 220km (136 miles); Biking Time: 16–20 hours/2 days

Ride out the Arniko Highway along the old route to Tibet. Head to Dhulikhel to view the sunset. At the crack of dawn aim for the Tibetan border descending to the Sun Kosi (River of Gold); climb to Barabise and on to Kodari, which marks the border of Tibet, and Friendship Bridge. Return the same route.

This is a make-it-or-bust trip, with lots of distance to cover on rough road. I particularly recommend employing support services of a bike touring company for this ride.

If you feel like Greg Lemond and know that you are not only in top shape but can bear hours on the saddle, you can make this race to the border in one day. I recommend two days however, spending the first night at Dhulikhel and riding to Kodari and back to Kathmandu the next. If you run out of steam at Kodari you can always flop at a modest lodge there, but do not expect much.

Remember that this is not the Tour-de-France but a vacation in Nepal. A comfortable pace avails you the camaraderie of the road and leaves you to enjoy the fantastic scenery.

Start any time of day from Kathmandu and ride 2 hours to **Dhulikhel** (see *Hike Itinerary 17*). The next day leave early and cruise downhill 37km (22 miles) to **Dolalghat** where the two mighty rivers, the **Sun Kosi** and **Indrawati**, converge to create a river runner's dream.

Rafting at Sun Kosi

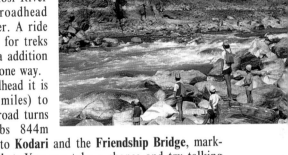

The road climbs out of the river gorge and runs high alongside the Sun Kosi River reaching the **Jiri** roadhead 16km (10 miles) later. A ride to Jiri, the trailhead for treks into Solu, is an extra addition of 110km (68 miles) one way.

From the Jiri roadhead it is another 15km (9½ miles) to **Barabise** where the road turns to dirt and climbs 844m (2,769ft) northward to **Kodari** and the **Friendship Bridge**, marking the border of Tibet. You can take a chance and try talking your way onto the bridge – one foot over the middle means you have been in **Tibet** – but you will most likely be stopped by the Nepal Immigration checkpost, situated just beyond Kodari among a line of shanty shelters housing road construction crews. Road maintenance is a round-the-clock occupation in a mountain range as young as the Himalaya.

Take heart in the knowledge that many a 19th-century explorer risked life and limb to enter Tibet or even to gaze upon the snow-peaked mountains before you now.

Return to Kathmandu via the same route, allowing time to make it in daylight. If you cannot bear the thought of riding back, negotiate a lift atop a local bus or transport truck on Nepal's only road link with Tibet.

Between Nepal and China

Hike-itineraries

12. Bishankhu Narayan

Hiking Time: 3½ hours/half day

Climb from Lubhu in the southeast of the Valley and sit above Kotdhara village as you lunch and survey the Valley. Visit the sacred Bishankhu Narayan with its unique purifying properties, making this pleasant little walk all the more worthwhile.

This walk begins with a taxi ride to Lubhu and ends with a pick-up at Baregaon on the Godavari road. At Lubhu, send your driver off to meet you 3½ hours later, telling him clearly to wait at Baregaon, even if you take a little longer. Do not pay in advance but do agree on a fee.

The Newari village of **Lubhu** lies nestled between Bhaktapur and Godavari. Follow the road towards the eastern Valley rim, passing through odd geometries of brick kiln yards. From Lubhu, set out on foot toward **Sisneri** village, skirting clusters of homes with thatch or tile roofs over fragile-looking red mud walls. After leaving Sisneri, bear right at the first road junction. After 10 minutes

you will reach a clearing with a village clubhouse on the left. The route begins to climb the mountain to your right, going around and behind it. The undulating lines of distant rice paddies condense into a rich corduroy texture, forming a backdrop to the glimmer of water in the earthen furrows.

After approximately 15 minutes you reach **Lamatal**. Take a break at Ms Badankal's tea stall. Above Lamatal the road becomes a trail left of the water tap. At the next junction take the path to the right leading to a bamboo grove. You have started your ascent to the saddle.

At the next junction turn right, take a deep breath and aim vertical. Take your time and proceed at a slow even pace. Feel your heart rate increase and know that you are engaged in the healthiest physical activity possible – aerobic exercise. If you have a watch take your pulse for 15 seconds, multiply it by four to get your heart rate and check the chart on page 45.

The tiny houses of the village below will appear toy-like as you gain altitude. Knee-high scrub brush line a well-worn path. Remember the Nepali fondness for singsong as you stride along and be glad that it is not monsoon when it is all *'raato maato, cheeplo baato'*

(red clay, slippery way). Across the bowl below you can see a road that climbs steeply to the ridge and over to Panauti.

After an hour's climb from Sisneri you reach the saddle at 1,719m (5,640ft) with beautiful views of the pocket valley of Godavari. If you want to go to **Godavari Botanical Gardens**, turn left here and follow the trail down. Take a bearing every once in a while or stop and ask for directions.

Down to the left, the picturesque village of **Manedhara** sits against the backdrop of Phulchoki, Kathmandu Valley's highest peak at 2,762m (9,062ft). The route takes you instead to the right towards the Newari village of **Kotdhara**, heralded by a *pipal* and a *bahar* tree, the sacred arboreal married couple which always

Thatch and mud houses

signals a resting place for the weary. The buffalo-wallowing hole and bamboo groves are part of the typical landscape of this thoroughly rural Valley village. At the next trail T-junction turn right and go a short distance for a spectacular unobstructed view of the Himalaya with the Kathmandu Valley spread below it. Just below you at the 12 o'clock position is Lubhu, and at one o'clock is the famous temple of Changu Narayan.

Walk down a couple of terraced paddies if you need a quiet spot for mountain-gazing or up to one of the houses and ask to sit in their compound. They will most likely assent and eventually a curious family member will join you.

When it is time to tear yourself away, return to the T-junction and go straight on through it. The trail descends to a ridge with a water hole on the left and a water spigot on the right. You have a clear view of Baregaon at 11 o'clock in front of you. Take the trail

A makeshift rope swing

down and to your left, heading towards the tree-lined hilltop. Walk with caution, keeping the knees bent. Walking with a straight leg can give you a condition known as Sahib's Knee, an extreme pain behind the kneecap that renders you almost helpless. The name refers to the inverse relationship of social status and the ability to descend mountains gracefully.

Soon you will reach the temple of **Bishankhu Narayan**. According to Nepalese legend, it is here that Lord Shiva hid from the demon Bhasmasur, who had been granted a boon from Lord Vishnu that all living things touched by his hand would turn into ashes. Shiva appealed to Vishnu to intercede on his behalf and Vishnu tricked the demon to touch his own forehead, thus turning himself to the ashes which formed the adjacent hillock.

The temple is a natural cave in a rock fissure where special stones are worshipped. Inside there is a statue of Vishnu behind a protective curtain of chain mail. Carefully stepping down a tight spiral staircase you reach the ground level on which stands a statue of Hanuman, the monkey god. In Nepali folklore it is believed sinners cannot squeeze through the rock fissure. Those who can, purify themselves of all past misdeeds.

Happy family

Follow the main trail down, taking the road to your right to the village of Baregaon. At **Godamchaur**, join the players at the soccer field if you see a game in action. Young people are generally enthusiastically receptive to your participation and it is a great way to meet them. Do not, however, plunge into your pocket just because they play barefoot and there is no goal net. Handouts from foreigners tend to spawn a passive attitude and eventual resentment.

Re-enter urban Nepal by going straight at the hump in the road. At the outskirts of town is a large *pipal* tree covered with bougainvillaea. The road steps down a terraced slope to a river and up the other side through cultivated fields. During monsoon and again during fall you can witness the festive atmosphere of the harvesting activities. Because of the close proximity of the road and the fields, you can take candid photos without intruding. If you really want, ask to help with this ancient backbreaking task. I did, lasted only three hours and had a sore back for two weeks!

This road takes you into **Baregaon** where it meets the paved Godavari road. Just before this junction is a Tibetan rug factory on your right. The weavers are all Newari women, part of the booming rug industry in Nepal. If your taxi driver does not show up, don't panic. A minibus or big blue public bus will be by (buses run until 7pm) and you can take it to Kathmandu for Rs 2.

13. Gokarna Safari Park

When you can't take one more hopeful hawker of rugs, money-changing, carpets or tiger balm and want to forget that you're a stranger in a strange land, this is the walk for you. Play golf, ride an elephant or just enjoy the many trails.

The King and Queen of Nepal each have their own forests and both are open to the public. Years ago the forests were hunting grounds. The Queen's forest is Nagarjun and the King's is here at **Gokarna Safari Park**. They are now used mostly by the Nepalese public; the royal family visit them only occasionally.

Start the day with a leisurely breakfast in the charming Rana cottage garden of **Mike's Breakfast**, located behind the Hotel Sherpa off Durbar Marg. Enjoy fresh orange juice and waffles with yoghurt accompanied by classical music.

Getting to Gokarna will cost approximately Rs 50 one way from

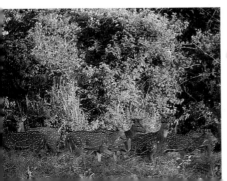

Cheetal deer at Gokarna

Breakfast at Mike's

downtown Kathmandu by taxi, the ride taking about 40 minutes. Pack a picnic lunch – there is also a restaurant here – and stroll to your heart's content.

Gokarna offers a quick getaway into clean quiet forest and solitude. You do not have to worry about being trampled by a rhino, mauled by a sloth bear or taken for dinner by a tiger. You will only be watched by deer that roam freely in herds throughout the park. There are footpaths for tramping through the forests and dirt roads for ambling amongst tall trees. Besides deer, there are monkeys, sometimes a caged tiger, and many species of birds. Maps are provided with the entry fee of Rs 25.

Sit with a box lunch and watch the monkeys run away to the amazement of the uninitiated golfer. Yes, the park even has a 9-hole golf course. Or try a round yourself for only Rs 500 which includes green fees, clubs, balls, tees and a caddy. You can also take an hour long elephant ride through the jungle for only US$7. Due to an odd quirk of rules, those with tourist visas must pay for their elephant ride in hard currency.

Upon leaving the park, either take a 20-minute walk to Bodhnath and catch a taxi back from there, or get a taxi at the park's gate and ask the driver to take you for a quick trip to **Gokarna Mahadev Temple** located northeast of Bodhnath (see *Bike Itinerary 2*). If you keep your temple visit to a half hour, the taxi rental should be about Rs 200, including the trip back to Kathmandu.

Bicycle rickshaws can cost more than taxis!

Hiking Time: 3–5 hours/half day

Hike up Nagarjun mountain through the densely forested Rani Ban (Queen's Forest). Reach the summit amidst swirling prayer flags and spectacular views of the Valley. Return the same route or scramble down the steeper southern side into the quiet valley of Ichangu.

Arrange a taxi to take you to **Nagarjun** gate (see *Bike Itinerary 1*). If you plan to descend the same route, depending on time, either arrange for the taxi to return and wait, or plan to walk about 1km (½ mile) to Balaju where taxis are available. If you descend via Ichangu you can usually get a taxi at the Ring Road-Swayambhunath crossroads. The latter walk is not recommended during the monsoon season or for the less-experienced.

The entry fee to the forest is 50 paisa per person. The trailhead is signed but ask the guard for directions if you cannot locate it. The beginning section follows steep steps cut into the hillside up to a clearing – a good rest spot. Follow a clear trail to the summit through oaks, rhododendrons and *chilaune*, a common mid-hill broad-leaf tree. Where the path crosses the road you will be greeted by strings of five-coloured prayer flags, at first just dancing over the crest and then as you reach the top becoming a thick fluttering canopy overhead. Unfortunately, the abundance above is matched by a pronounced litter of paper at your feet, much of it tiny block-prints of Buddhist deities scattered in religious fervour.

Nagarjun summit

The summit has a *stupa* and *dharmasala* (resthouse) for overnight pilgrims, though there is no water up here. Climb up the spiral viewing tower to get a better view of the Kathmandu Valley (see *Bike Itinerary 1* to identify the northern peaks). Relax a while on this holy hilltop where no doubt the great Tibetan sage Nagarjuna came to take an occasional break from his meditation retreat in the caves below.

For the intrepid and experienced trekker who does not want to duplicate tracks, leave the Nagarjun summit via the steep southern side for a 2-hour return to Ring Road. Go to the edge away from the tower and follow the trail down to the two picnic pavilions. At the second one, the trail descent begins, although not well-defined at first. Take a reading from the top and know that you are heading down a ridge on a woodcutters' and pilgrims' trail. Try to stay on this ridge line rather than cut down the steep sides.

You quickly reach forest where the trail is still steep but clear. This is too slippery for a monsoon descent. Cross the dirt Rani Ban road and continue down through the trees reaching a village of Gurung and Magar hill people and the Newars of the Valley.

Just after passing an abandoned and broken-roofed temple, the trail reaches the Valley floor at the dirt road to Ichangu. You can turn right (adding ½ hour) and visit the **Ichangu Narayan** temple if you haven't seen it already (see *Bike Itinerary 4*) and then backtrack to Ring Road.

Primula bloom

Hail a taxi or walk around Swayambhunath (see *Day 1*) and into Thamel for a savoury pizza or a plate of rich gnocchi at **La Cimbaldi**, an Italian restaurant located on the main Thamel shopping street up from Thahiti Tole.

15. Thankot To Kirtipur

Hiking Time: 3–4 hours/half day

This level little hike starts from Thankot, a village way-station southwest of Kathmandu, on the old walking trail from the Terai lowlands into the Valley. Walk through fields and villages in the southern foothills, heading for Maccha Narayan temple. End your walk at Kirtipur, the last Newari kingdom to fall to King Prithvi Narayan Shah in 1769.

Take a taxi 30 minutes out of town to **Thankot**, a police checkpoint and westernmost village on the highway leaving the Valley. Start your walk between the police post and the white **Bagwati Temple**, guarded by an outrageous pair of lions painted green in private places.

The trail starts narrow then widens, leading to a Y-intersection

Kirtipur terraces

Matatirtha Temple

next to a *dhara* (waterspout). Turn right and uphill to a **Shiva Temple** with its venerated stone and old ruins. Head towards a small *stupa*.

You will be contouring a series of small shoulders jutting out from the southern Valley hills, Bhasmasur and Champa Devi. This trail stays in the fields and villages to enjoy the local colour; there is also an optional higher route in the foothills. Your path heads for the village of **Macchegaon**, home to Maccha Narayan. It twists and turns a bit; if you lose the way, just ask and you will eventually reach your destination.

This is a good trek for trying out new Nepali words or for chatting with English-speakers met on the way. As in most Valley villages, you will meet an engaging friendliness that is neither pushy nor shy – a sign that you are out of the city and not on a tourist route. After the *stupa* the trail turns right in front of a large typical Nepali farmhouse. Take the small paddy bund leading left directly away from the front of the house. When the grains have grown tall the bund will be harder to pick out.

Stay on this path heading straight for the electric tower in the distance. After you cross over two stone slabs, turn left and right again after a few minutes. You are now on the main trail heading for Macchegaon.

Walk through the next intersection and at the T-junction turn right and uphill to a large field with a school on the left. To your right is **Matatirtha Temple** where in April–May thousands of women gather to celebrate Mother's Day.

Follow the road across the bridge and up to the right to an open field with a *pipal* tree, *chautara* (stone seat) and *paathi*

Picking valley vegetables

Kirtipur street

(resthouse) on your right; go right of the *pipal* tree.

Stay on the trail as it climbs up and down, intersecting small jeepable roads. Pass through a field with a small piped *dhara* (waterspout) to the right. Walk past two cement-plastered communal *chaarpis* (outhouses) and applaud this sign of sanitation development. Just beyond them the trail climbs up from the field.

After a while you will reach a *dhara* under a large *bahar* tree with a stone deity and a *paathi* to the left. The trail goes left and passes below the 1953 USAID-funded ropeway. Supplies are ferried to and from the Terai on this inexpensive, low-tech and minimal impact mode of transportation. Sadly, road transport has won the day and is consequently fouling the air of this perfect valley bowl.

After the ropeway, the trail goes up along the left side of the small house on the hill. It turns right at the corner of the house and left heading directly away from the house. At the T-junction turn left and head towards the *pipal* tree. Walk down some tricky steps in the wall and turn right into the clearing. The *pipal* tree is a great picnic lunch spot and if you are lucky you might find some activity in this favourite kite flying area. Here, you are on the outskirts of Macchegaon, just 10 minutes away.

Continue across the field, skip the first right at the big stone and follow the next right into Macchegaon village. Turn right at the first village street and head toward the Vishnu temple of **Maccha Narayan**. Every third year, thousands of people come to worship at

Macha Narayan's garuda

this temple and *pokhari* (pond) complex representing Vishnu's incarnation as a fish.

To leave Macchegaon village, go back to where you entered but continue straight (north) to a stone arch where you turn right and head downhill out of the village. From here you can see the ridge city of **Kirtipur** sitting upon twin hillocks with the majestic Himals in the background.

Take the left fork of the first trail junction and go right at the next junction, past a house surrounded by trees and a bamboo grove. The trail snakes up and down terraced rice paddies and all trails from here lead to Kirtipur. Approaching the town from the south, where less urbanisation has occurred, allows you to experience a bit of the expansive paddy fields that once filled the Kathmandu Valley.

Originally part of Patan, Kirtipur gained an interim of independence as a fourth kingdom until the lengthy siege staged by Prithvi Narayan Shah, the king from Gorkha. The Kirtipurians fought so fiercely and taunted the Gorkha forces so that Prithvi, in vengeance, had the noses cut off all males except those who played wind instruments.

Enter the town by going straight up the hillock towards the upper end on your left. Make your way to the **Kvath Temple** on the highest western point of Kirtipur. The temple is dedicated to Uma Maheshwar (Shiva with his consort, Uma) and a pair of elephants sit at the top of the steps guarding the lovers. From here you can survey the rest of Kirtipur.

The Chilanchu Vihar stupa

Wind back down the main street past a beautiful window with five bays over a doorway to **Lyaku**, part of the old palace. Make your way to the famous **Bagh Bhairav Temple** in the middle of town where weapons seized by Prithvi Narayan Shah from the decisive 1769 battle still hang on the temple walls. Head south to **Dev Phuki**, the large, deep pond surrounded by a group of beautiful houses clustered on terraces.

Climb up through the narrow streets to the **Chilanchu Vihar** *stupa*, built in the form of Swayambhunath in 1514 atop the southern hill. Drop down the stairs behind the *stupa* towards **Naya Bazaar** and beyond to the bus stop where you can catch a bus or taxi into town.

Cap this day off fittingly with a Newari meal featuring marinated meats, beans and spicy vegetable dishes served with steamed or beaten rice *(chyura)*, at the **Thayabhu Newar Restaurant** (Tel: 411570), located at the Lotus Plaza off Lazimpat.

Hiking Time: 6 hours/full day

Head south out of the city toward Dakshinkali. At Pikhel walk up to the Himalayan Heights Resort at Hatiban for tea and a breathtaking panoramic view. Walk on up to Champa Devi, return for lunch at the resort and amble back down to your taxi for the ride back.

Arrange with your hotel for a taxi for a round trip to Pikhel (about 40 minutes) and a 4–5 hour wait. Cost should be in the region of Rs 600, the full day rate for a private taxi. Not all taxis can make it up the steep dirt road, so discuss this with the driver.

Get out at **Pikhel** at the dirt road to **Himalayan Heights Resort** (Tel: 221129, 221181), also known as **Hatiban** (Elephant Woods),

Champa Devi's pine wood

the local name for the area, and tell the driver to wait for you. The turning is marked by a white sign on a concrete electric pole on the right side of the main Dakshinkali road. The walk to the hotel takes about 45 minutes.

Enjoy the mountain lodge architecture of this four-star hotel set in an idyllic pine forest. From its garden, study the splendour of the mountains, taking in the mighty peaks, from Himalchuli in the west to Everest on the east. You will not find any better accommodation and views than this.

The 1½–2 hour hike to the summit of **Champa Devi** (2,278m/7,474ft) follows the graded dirt road that takes off from the resort going west for 10 minutes and then joins a walking trail.

From here you will walk the ridge-line of **Neupane Dara** with the Kathmandu Valley and Himalaya on your right and a small valley headed by **Doldu** village on your left. The ascent starts gradually, soon leaving the forested ridge behind and progressing to a stiffer slope. Traverse the south side until the trail drops down to a saddle before making the final climb to the summit. The true summit of Champa Devi is marked by a small white *stupa* with commanding views of the Valley. In the southwest corner of the

Scanning the horizon from Champa Devi

Valley you can see Thankot, the start of *Hikes 15* and *21*, to Kirtipur and Hetauda. You can also catch glimpses of Pharping and Dakshinkali. If you continue another hour you will reach **Bhasmasur** peak (2,545m/8,349ft) gaining 267m (875ft), and crossing one more saddle to reach there.

It is an hour's walk down from Champa Devi to the hotel. The first section is a steep descent, so watch your step. If you want to gaze at something or take photographs, please stop walking! People have fallen off trails because they fail to stop while enjoying the wonderful panorama.

Making offerings at the Kali Temple

From the hotel it is a 30-minute descent to Pikhel and your waiting taxi for the ride back to Kathmandu. Or, if you are up for a bit more temple watching, persuade your driver to take you several kilometres down the road to the important **Kali Temple** at Dakshinkali where on Tuesdays and Saturdays Hindus make animal sacrifices to this bloodthirsty goddess. It is also a popular picnic ground. Stop on your way back at the Buddhist monastery at **Pharping** where Guru Rinpoche is said to have performed miraculous flying feats, leaving his footprints behind. You may have to pay the driver another Rs 100 for this extra leg.

17. Namo Buddha

Hiking Time: 8 hours/full day

Take a taxi or bus to Dhulikhel in time to catch the sunset splashed over the Himalayan horizon. Head out early the next morning for your walk to the Buddhist pilgrimage site of Namo Buddha. Stroll back to Dhulikhel via Sankhu and Batase, well-heeled farming and trading villages.

Sunset from Dhulikhel

If you choose to stay overnight I recommend either the. **Himalayan Horizon Hotel Sun N Snow** (Tel: 011 61114; single US$45, double US$50) or **Dhulikhel Lodge** (Tel: 011 61296; single US$1.40, double US$2.23) depending on your budget. The former, located off the highway before Dhulikhel, comprises three traditional style buildings grouped around a commodious garden. The latter is in Dhulikhel proper and gives you a feel of village life and the warmth of trekker camaraderie. Plan for an early breakfast and be on the road by 7.30am so that you don't have to feel your way back in the dark. Bring a packed lunch, plenty of water and extra clothes in case the weather changes.

Enter the compact Newari town of **Dhulikhel** if you are staying at the Himalayan Horizon, once a thriving trade post levying taxes on traffic between east Nepal, Kathmandu and Tibet. The wealth of woodcarving evident on homes is testimony to a previous prosperity levied as gold from traders.

Turn right at the first T-junction. Pass the famous low-budget **Dhulikhel Lodge** on your left and keep going straight to visit the **Bhagvati Temple** with its three-tiered roof and the several shrines

The stupa at Namo Buddha

to Shiva close by. Retrace your steps back, past your entry road and continue straight (east) when you reach the pond. This new end of town has abandoned the graceful brick and tile traditional building forms for modern concrete plastered boxes.

Twenty minutes beyond the pond the paved road turns to dirt and angles right uphill. Immediately beyond the turn, a walking trail splits off up and to the left of the dirt track. The footpath goes more or less straight up, crisscrossing the road for the first few hours.

At the first road crossing, a small shop sits in a natural hollow under tree roots. The merchant sells oranges if in season, or sweets for your all-day hike. On your left are concrete steps to a **Kali Temple** atop a small hill.

Continue along the trail down through Chhetri and Brahman homes to the road. Follow the walking trail immediately to your left and down through the village of **Kavre**. Meet with the road again at a large *pipal* tree and a *chautara* (stone seat) and continue to the left.

After 10 minutes and another *chautara*, a walking trail splits off left from the road, heading straight up through pine forest. This area was heavily reforested with the help of the Australian government, which has given highly successful support to Nepal's forests.

View from Dhulikhel

The trail returns to the road again which you now follow all the way to Namo Buddha. Stop at the Tamang village of **Phulbari** for a tea break. A bit further along, the road forks just below two small tastefully modernised Nepalese-style buildings – creating something like a European chalet. Take the road to your right leading to Namo Buddha hill.

At the base of the hill, marked by two electric poles, turn right and climb up to the **Namo Buddha** *stupa*. Together with the shrines at the top, this is one of the eight most holy pilgrimage sites that every Buddhist must visit in a lifetime.

According to Nepalese legend, Buddha lived as a prince in nearby Panauti in a previous lifetime. One day, the prince and his brothers went on a hunting trip into the hills where they encountered a starving tigress and her cubs. The compassionate prince offered his own body to save the animals' lives. When the tigress refused, he cut off his flesh and fed her with his own hands. The family enshrined his remains in the lower *stupa*, and the site of the actual sacrifice has been marked by a small *stupa* and stone image on top of the hill.

There are two Tibetan *gompas* (monasteries) on the hillside be-

The tree shop is a local landmark

decked with a flurry of prayer flags. Recently, a colossal 2.4-m (8-ft) tall Buddha was added to the summit. Find yourself a little niche and eat your lunch.

Walk down to the lower *stupa* and exit by the large prayer wheel. Turn left down the road and take the walking trail that splits off to the left. Follow it to the white Shiva temple and Durga shrine. Continue into the Newari village of **Sankhu**. Just to the right, after the small bridge and behind a low house is a lovely old *paathi* (resthouse). Follow the main road until it turns left at a sign saying 'Way to Panauti'; angle right and downhill instead, unless you would rather go to Panauti. If you do, continue along the road for about an hour and catch a bus from Panauti back to Dhulikhel or Kathmandu.

Stay to the right at the next Y-intersection, going downhill and passing through the fertile fields of the valley floor. The area is called Sankhu and each village has a derivative form of the name. This string of little urbanised villages is full of well-preserved old brick edifices with several exceptionally finely carved *paathis*, well-kept and full of life.

Keep your eyes open for a silversmith named **Ratna Kagi Sakya**, and stop to see his handiwork. His home is on the right beyond the chicken house in the last of the Sankhu villages. In the middle of the road is an elegant Ganesh shrine. Where the road forks go right and uphill past a lovely woodcarved *paathi* on your left. The straight fork is another way to Panauti.

Leave the Newars behind and climb into the Chhetri village of **Batase.** At the Y-intersection turn left and follow the hillside contour until you reach a footpath spur on your right going 6m (20ft)

Newari farmstead below Namo Buddha

up to a ridge with a single large tree on top. Follow the path down 150m (500ft) through brush and across a small stream.

At the second stream go straight and on the other side of the field take the left fork which winds upward to enter Dhulikhel from the western edge of town near the Bhagvati Temple. Turn right and back to the main entrance to town. If no taxis are available, you should be able to catch a stuffed-as-sardines bus – no exaggeration – back to Kathmandu. If not, there is always the Dhulikhel Lodge.

18. Shivapuri

Hiking Time: 7 hours/full day

Climb the Valley's second highest mountain, Shivapuri. Take a hike complete with village life, a Buddhist monastery, virgin oak and rhododendron forests and grand mountain views. You may also choose to visit the source of the Bagmati River and the hermitage of Swami Chandresh, located near the top of Shivapuri.

Trekking in fairy tale-like forests

Make sure you read about food, water and nutrition and stock up before starting on this hike. Take a taxi north up the Maharajgunj Road, straight across the Ring Road and through Bansbari to the village of **Budhanilkantha** at the foot of **Shivapuri** mountain. It will take about ½ hour from the centre of Kathmandu.

From Budhanilkantha, the route by road or trail heads northeast up to **Nage Gompa**, the Buddhist monastery partway up the mountain. If you choose the road, take the taxi another 10 minutes up the hill, past the Reclining Vishnu Temple, to the gate of the **Shivapuri Watershed and Wildlife Preserve** where you will start your walk. Take the first right after the gate. You will soon see **Nage Gompa** high on a ridge before you. Below the monastery, watch for the well-worn trail cut into the slope on your left. It will be approximately 1 hour from the gate.

My recommendation for the more intrepid is to head off the road and traverse up the inhabited slopes toward Nage Gompa. Leaving

Village wedding procession

your taxi at the Reclining Vishnu Temple, turn north. At the first road on your right, turn and go east over the bridge onto a dirt track. It contours the base of the mountain, taking you through Tamang villages with views of the Valley below. The prayer flags blowing from bamboo poles tell you that this is a Buddhist community. There are innumerable paths so keep inquiring the direction to the *gompa*. Do not assume the intended path and point, as the polite response from villagers is to say yes to wherever you point.

Just past a white *stupa* with a small Buddha, the trail turns north at a metal electric pole, then right again and across a small creek with a large stone slab bridge. Do not go over the bridge, but straight up the mountain.

You will be passing through front yards of houses and should be respectful, but need not be embarrassed about trespassing. Some sections dwindle to mere goat trails, which are tricky without split hooves. Imagine carrying a heavy load up these steep hills during monsoon or fetching water daily, as many of the women do.

Remember to take your bearings on a distant house or boulder. The trail climbs up with small eastward traverses and reaches a house where men make *khukris*, the traditional Nepalese knife. Just below you will see two small *stupas* and a broken down section of the Shivapuri Water Project wall. Cross it and continue up towards a destroyed building, passing to the right of two small *stupas*. You will go through a small, shady pine grove just before the trail reaches the road. Turn left at the road and take the monastery steps on the right.

This is a good place to take your bearings. Check out the other roads on the mountain. You can see Tokha Hospital to the west and the roads leading to it from above and below, both rideable (see *Bike Itinerary 7*).

To proceed to the summit, climb up the steps to Nage Gompa. Above the monastery there are many prayer flags which mark the trail. It is best to start your Shivapuri climb right by the water tap. The trail is initially steep and deeply rutted, but gets easier.

Between the monastery and the ridge line you will pass three trail junctions; stay to the left at each. Just before the second junction you will reach an abandoned field and house. Beyond the shoulder ridge you will pass another junction. Stay to the left and within 10 minutes you will reach a meadow, the usual lunch stop and sometimes overnight halt for this trek, with good views of Dorje Lakpa peak. Immediately beyond the meadow the main trail branches off to the left, but you take the trail to the right to **Bagdwar**, the source of the holy Bagmati River. It is also the route to the hermitage of Swami Chandresh.

Keep to the left at the first two trail junctions. The trail takes you through a thick virgin forest of moss-covered oak and rhododendron trees; one of the few of its kind in the Valley. In spring, this forest becomes God's slide show. The thick canopy of red rhododendron blossoms is kaleidoscopic and the ground will be blanketed red. As you gain altitude the flowers fade in colour; from a worldly red to pure white.

The trail contours the mountain and just before **Bagdwar Gompa** crosses a small spring above a pond. This is the sacred source of the holiest river in Nepal, the Bagmati River which runs through Pashupatinath. Unfortunately, the maintenance of this sacred spring was neglected when the local inhabitants were relocated with the establishment of the Shivapuri Wildlife Preserve; today, the spring lies in ruin.

A little further along is the newly restored **Bagdwar Gompa**, inhabited by a silent monk. This was also in ruins until a few years ago. Next to the water tap is a worn path; from here it is a 35-minute walk straight up to the summit of **Shivapuri** (2,732m/8,963ft).

If you want to meet the **Swami Chandresh** you should instead

Bagmati River source near the summit of Shivapuri

Swami Chandresh

turn right at the water tap and take the trail for 25 minutes up to his hermitage. The trail crosses a brook, goes up a small rise and becomes quite soggy. At the crest of this rise follow the trail to your left heading towards a large tree. The trail enters a small open meadow and continues up from the right hand corner. You reach a saddle at a T-junction. Turn right to the Swami's hermitage; after your visit, return and go left for a 25-minute climb up the ridge to Shivapuri.

Some know the Swami as the Shivapuri Baba but he prefers not to be called that in deference to the renowned Shivapuri Baba who lived here for many years and who died in 1963 at the age of 137. Swami Chandresh has been living on top of Shivapuri for the past two decades. At the request of his followers, this Hindu sage started a primary school, Budhanilkantha Ashram School, with a curriculum addressing physical, mental, and spiritual well-being.

The summit of Shivapuri commands a spectacular view of Ganesh Himal (7,111m/22,755ft), Langtang Lirung (7,245m/23,184ft), and Dorje Lakpa (6,966m/22,291ft). This is a popular spot and you may find that many happy campers have reached it before you. If so, and you want solitude, you can try the northwest corner beyond the military compound.

For an adventurous descent, leave the summit via the southwest corner. Pass by the military compound and take care as you start a very steep descent. This is where a walking stick will come in handy.

Just down from the top the trail butts into a huge boulder that is accessible from the high side. You can sit here and enjoy a beautiful view of the valley north of the Shivapuri and Ganesh Himal massifs. My philosophy is not to conquer Shivapuri by seeing how

Looking north from Shivapuri towards Tibet

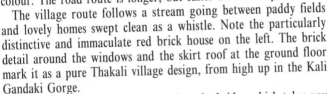

fast you can go up or down, but to enjoy its many beautiful sights, pausing to make connections with nature.

Continue down and stay left at two trail junctions. The trail is steep, rocky and slippery in places so take your time. You are still hours away from the city and a sprained ankle is a needless Himalayan experience.

After almost 2 hours you will reach the dirt road that circles part way around Shivapuri mountain. Here you have a choice of turning left and staying on the road all the way back to Budhanilkantha or to continue straight down the trail and through the villages. If you can handle more of the steep downhill, I recommend the village route for more local colour. The road route is longer, but easier on the body.

The village route follows a stream going between paddy fields and lovely homes swept clean as a whistle. Note the particularly distinctive and immaculate red brick house on the left. The brick detail around the windows and the skirt roof at the ground floor mark it as a pure Thakali village design, from high up in the Kali Gandaki Gorge.

The trail runs into the paved road at the bridge which takes you to the bus stop beside the Reclining Vishnu Temple where you started your walk. Watch on your left for Swami Chandresh's **Budhanilkantha Ashram School** and pay a visit if you have time. At the bus stop you can take a minibus or public bus (last bus departs at 5pm) back to Kathmandu or a private taxi if you have arranged one beforehand. Sometimes metered taxis are available.

19. Godavari to Phulchoki

Hiking Time: 6–8 hours/full day

A hike to the top of Phulchoki, highest of the Valley rim peaks, rewards the hardy hiker with far-stretching views. During spring, this forested hill brightens with crimson rhododendrons, scented daphne and a myriad of wild flowers; thus its name 'flower covered hill'. This hike is no Sunday stroll; be ready for strenuous ups and downs on a well-worn path beginning at Godavari, 20km (13 miles) southeast of Kathmandu. Alternatively, you can bike the entire route from Kathmandu.

Perhaps the most economical and efficient transport to **Godavari** is by taxi (about Rs 250). All taxi drivers know this approximately ½-hour drive leaving the Ring Road from its southeast quadrant. When you return, catch a local bus from Godavari back to Patan's Lagankhel bus station, where you can get a taxi to Kathmandu. Mini and blue buses run daily every ½–1 hour from Godavari until 7pm.

Bike Ride: A partly paved dirt-gravel road leads to the top of Phulchoki from Godavari. There is little vehicular traffic on the mountain except on Saturdays. Hard-core experienced bikers could do this long and extremely strenuous ride in minimum 9 hours from Kathmandu, round-trip. Plan on a good 4–5 hours climb from Godavari up to the top; the upper gravel stretches are particularly challenging. There is no water en route so bring plenty.

The Hike: Two hiking trails lead to the top of Phulchoki mountain (2,762m/9,062ft) gaining more than 1,200m (4,000ft) from the elevated Valley floor. Out of concern for trekkers' knees, the following route takes the steeper path up, and the gentler one down but it could be done in reverse. A walking stick helps brace the knees for steep descents and can be found in Thamel in trekking shops. Good hiking boots are also in order – remember to lace them up tight for the downhill to prevent blisters – and a warm sweater or jacket as temperatures cool considerably at the top. Expect to encounter snow on high ground as late as early February.

Ask the taxi driver to drop you at the **Phulchoki Shrine**, about 100m (300ft) up the road from St Xavier's School on the left. Enter the temple compound via a stone walkway from the road. A sister temple to that on top the mountain, the shrine honours the mother goddess Phulchoki Mai, one of the numerous female divinities of the Valley.

Exit the temple north, opposite the quarried hillside, the source of Godavari's coveted pink marble. A well-worn path leads up into the bush, curving right. After gaining a little altitude, glance back towards Kathmandu with Ganesh and Langtang Himals peaks barely visible through the haze. Gaining slightly more, look north at the next ridge and see your return trail zigzagging down the hill.

After 30 minutes of walking you enter an oak and rhododendron forest which will ac-

Laligurans flower in spring

company you to the top. Here, beginning in February at lower reaches up until April higher up, Nepal's national flower, the *laligurans* (*Rhododendron arboreum*) blooms in abundance.

Stay on the main trail heading upward, steep in places and paralleling electrical wires. After 45 minutes, you will cross a wide level path; ignore it. After an hour, you will cross the road for the first time, then a second, and so on. Continue on the trail crossing the road seven or eight times. Wherever the continuation trail is not immediately apparent, walk up the road a few minutes and look for it on the opposite bank.

At about the ninth crossing, a scrambler trail leaves from the left of the curve near a large square concrete hole in the road. Take this short steep trail. After reaching the road, stay on it for a couple of bends, passing a row of concrete blocks which serve as barriers on the left. It is harder to see the trail beginnings so keep a constant lookout on the uphill side; or you can just stay on the road the rest of the way for about an hour.

At last you will see the radio tower and military buildings marking the summit. There is a small *chorten* for Buddhist worshippers, and a cluster of tridents and vermilion-stained rocks marking the **Phulchoki Mai** site. Find a comfortable spot for a well-deserved picnic lunch and take in the view north of the Himalaya and the eastern Kathmandu Valley ringed with hills. To the south, blue hillcrests stretch into the haze towards the Terai lowlands and India.

Count your daylight hours, saving 2–3 hours to get down, depending on how fast you walk. Head down the same road you came up for about 40 minutes, and watch to your right in the distance below for a clear trail leading north along the ridge line. You will see it for

Practise patience with curious kids

several minutes and a few road bends before you leave the road on a sketchy trail dropping steeply from the right edge. You meet the main trail in a few minutes, and should keep left at the first junction. Head generally west. Go right at the next two trail junctions, and soon the hillside will open up as you leave forest cover. On the ridge to the left you will be able to see the electrical lines that

95

paralleled you on the way up.

Continue heading west, through oak and rhododendron groves and soon Kathmandu comes into view. You cross a tempting, wide level path at the crest of this hill, but continue straight on the eroded path down and to the left, descending to the round buildings you saw this morning. Pass the building on the right and reach the paved road where you started this morning. Turn right, down to the tea shops beyond St Xavier's School. Have a cup of tea and some biscuits while waiting for the bus, or if you are lucky, an empty taxi. If time permits and you have energy left, wander over to the **Royal Botanical Gardens** (open daily 10am–5pm) and enter by paying a nominal charge. You pass the **Department of Medicinal Plants** and might inquire the way to **Godavari Kunda**, a temple where sacred waters are believed connected by underground channels to the Godavari River in South India. The tale of an Indian *yogi* who lost his staff and bowl when bathing in South India and found them here is proof enough!

A Hindu holy man

On the drive back to Kathmandu you will pass through red brick villages where garlands of chillies, garlic and cauliflower leaves hang drying from rafters. At Baregaon, a dirt road leads north to Bishankhu Narayan (see *Hike Itinerary 12*) and another south to Vajra Varahi and Chapagaon Village (see *Bike Itinerary 6*). No matter how crowded the bus might be, it will feel good to be off your feet.

20. Nagarkot to Shivapuri

Hiking Time: 14–16 hours/2–3 Days

Long after the Himalaya rose from beneath the Tethys Sea to become the highest mountain range on earth, a fresh-water lake filled the Kathmandu Valley. A 2–3 day walk along the northern Valley rim from Nagarkot to Shivapuri overlooks this legend-filled bowl and reveals unexpected panoramas of the snow-draped Himals, seemingly close enough to touch. Use a reputable trek agent to handle the camping and guide arrangements.

This hike can be done in either 2 or 3 days, depending on whether you camp a second night at Shivapuri or descend to Budhanilkantha late on the second day. I highly recommend the former, so that you can wake up to one of the grandest Himalayan sunrise sights you can imagine.

You start the hike at **Nagarkot**, reached by foot in about 5 hours, by taxi (1hr) or bus (2–3hrs) from Bhaktapur. You should spend the night in Nagarkot, either camping outdoors or staying in

The 'hillstation' of Nagarkot

a lodge (see *Bike Itinerary 8*) to get an early start.

The next day is a full day so start walking by 7.30 or 8.00am. From Nagarkot you can see much of the **Kattike** and **Manicur Dara** ridges, extending north and northwest, which you will follow to Shivapuri, north of Kathmandu. From the Vajra Farmhouse, exit down the driveway and turn right. Descend on this dirt road for about 20 minutes till you come to a fork. Go right – the left fork leads down to Sankhu, described in *Bike Itinerary 8*. Following the graded road you contour the hillside reaching **Chauki Bhanjyang** in several hours. You might stop for lunch here. Then climb a bit and stay below the ridge alternating between road and trail, open scrub and oak and rhododendron forests for the rest of the day.

Your destination tonight is **Chisopani** (Cold Water) village, located off the ridge to the north. The trekking staff will have set up camp before you arrive; hot tea and snacks will be waiting. All you have to do is stretch out and take in the fresh air; at night stars sparkle from this elevated vantage. Such are the joys of trekking, far from life's worries. There are no lodges here so if you are hiking on your own without food or tent, you will have to continue on another 90 minutes or so to **Burlang Bhanjyang** (2,438m/8,000ft).

The next morning you will climb back northwest to the ridge-top, meeting the **Sundarijal-Helambu trail**, a busy trade corridor between Kathmandu and the northern hills. Here you encounter travellers carrying potatoes or rice to market and new clothes and commodities back home. They may ask you '*Kahaa jaane?*' (Where are you going?) or '*Bhaat khayo?*'

The descent to Sundarijal can be hard on the knees

Sundarijal is one of Kathmandu's important water sources

enquiring whether you have eaten, the most common greetings between friends on the trail. This stretch is a notorious bandit hangout, so walk together and do not trek alone.

The trail now hugs the ridge-top all the way west to Shivapuri, opening to northern views over the Likhu Khola river and if clear, the Himalaya. Kathmandu appears a sprawling metropolis, as it is fast becoming with a burgeoning population of over one million. You pass a clearing with three *chortens* (Buddhist shrines) marking a holy spot.

From here the walk enters one of my favourite forests. Moss-draped giant oaks and rhododendrons shade a primeval environment. Stop now and then to observe the forest floor, watch for boar rooting and listen for the cheerful song of the bright sunbird. It is nice to carry a plastic litter bag whenever you are hiking and help clean up the trails. You can burn paper trash at camp and

A yellow mustard field

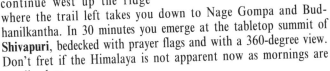

carry the rest back to the city.

About 2 hours beyond the *chortens*, you come to the clearing near where the Swami Chandresh lives (see *Hike Itinerary 18*). If you are spending the night atop Shivapuri, continue west up the ridge where the trail left takes you down to Nage Gompa and Budhanilkantha. In 30 minutes you emerge at the tabletop summit of **Shivapuri**, bedecked with prayer flags and with a 360-degree view. Don't fret if the Himalaya is not apparent now as mornings are usually clear.

Rise before dawn and get out, yes all the way out of your tent for an unforgettable sunrise. From far left in the misty distance you may see **Annapurna II** with its snow-capped charcoal grey roof line. Moving eastward, pick out pointed **Himalchuli**, then **Ganesh Himal**'s three sisters, and the white pyramid of **Langtang Lirung** rising behind the lava black ridge of **Gosainkund** centrestage. Next is **Dorje Lakpa**, like an inverted shark tooth, and prominent **Gauri Shanker**.

If it is exceptionally clear, you can see **Numbur** just to the right of a distant U-shaped dip, and further east, with cloud breath blowing from its tiny dark summit, **Mount Everest**.

Turning to look down on sprawling Kathmandu; you may wish you were staying here another night. At your leisure, descend one of two trails to Budhanilkantha in about 3–4 hours (see *Hike Itinerary 18*).

21. Thankot to Daman

Distance (Thankot to Kulikhani): 32km (20 miles); Hiking Time: 8 hours; Biking Distance (Thankot to Daman): 48½km (30 miles); Biking Time: 6 hours; Total: 3 days

The historic trade route that linked India, Nepal, Tibet and China takes you out of the southwest corner of the Valley through Thankot. It gives you one night in the forest and another with a 400-km (250-mile) view at the Everest Panorama Resort. Start this 3-day trip on foot and end it on wheels. Make arrangements with Himalayan Mountain Bikes.

Organise with **Himalayan Mountain Bikes** (Tel: 411724) for a trekking guide and porters to take you from Thankot to Kulikhani and for bikes to

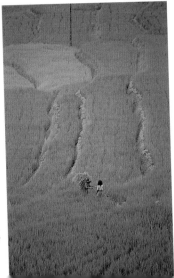

Verdant rice fields

Working buffalo hide

be waiting for the second segment of your trip. The route is also bikeable for the hardcore, except for a 2-hour push/carry stint up the mountain to Chandagiri Pass. If you are lucky, you will find some children willing to carry your bikes for a fee of about Rs 100.

As early as 600BC this trail linked Nepal and China with the north Indian trade route to Uttarapatha. With the establishment of the Tibetan nation in the 8th century this became the passage of choice for trade and pilgrimage among travellers.

Start out at **Thankot**, a village which dates back to Licchavi times. The trail winds through Newari and Tamang homes, climbing up the forested slopes to the **Chandragiri Pass** (2,280m/7,480ft). Stop and imagine being one of the 40 porters carrying a Rolls Royce over this steep trail before the Raj Path was built — the first of such cars arrived in 1900.

After reaching the saddle and *stupa* on top in 2–3 hours, continue down through **Chitlung** with its lovely carved *paathi* (resthouse) and *dhara* (waterspout). This old trail goes through now-secluded villages encircled by well-groomed fields, culminating at an especially lovely gorge above the **Kulikhani Dam**.

Your pre-arranged camp can be set up above the dam for a quiet evening of relaxation. The next day, hike the short distance to the roadhead where your sag wagon will be waiting with bikes, and mount up for the 1,028-m (3,374-ft) pedal up to **Daman** (see *Bike Itinerary 10*). The dirt road starts level then rises to the paved **Raj Path** highway just before Palung where you turn left to head for Daman.

At Daman, lock your bikes near one of the small restaurants and walk up to the Lookout Tower. You can see seven of the 10 highest mountains in the world. Return to your bikes and continue up the road for 3km (1¼ miles) to spend the night at Everest Panorama Resort (Tel: 415372).

The next morning you can return to Kathmandu by reversing the approach described in *Bike Itinerary 10*, or head further south to Hetauda and the excitement of the jungles of the Terai.

Right: repairing a flat

Practical Information

TRAVEL ESSENTIALS

When to Visit

October to April is the best time to visit Nepal, with temperatures of 10°C–25°C (50°F–77°F), sparkling sunny days and cold nights dropping to almost freezing. The cold clear winter months of December and January are good for mountain views, despite misty mornings and an invigorating evening chill.

The next best months for biking and hiking are February and March with spring flowers and gentle temperatures. Late April and May can be hot (11°C–30°C/52°F–86°F) and hazy and with occasional evening thunderstorms.

It is best to avoid the trails and dirt roads during monsoon rains from June to September. Although temperatures are down (19°C–36°C/66°F–97°F) intermittent violent downpours (often only at night) create some flooding and landslides, and humidity is high. On paved roads in the Valley, however, this can be one of the prettiest times with intermittent rain, lush green rice fields, and wonderful light effects.

Visas and Trekking Permits

Visas for 30 days can be obtained from a Nepalese Embassy in foreign countries prior to arrival. Visas valid for 15 days can be obtained on arrival at Kathmandu airport for US$40. The visa can be extended for up to three months at the Department of Immigration in Thamel, Tel 412337 (open 10am–5pm daily; until 3pm on Friday, closed Saturday) for no extra fee upon proof that at least US$20 per day has been exchanged at a bank or authorised money changer for the duration of the visit. You will not need a trekking permit for any of the bike rides or hikes described in this book, except for *Bike Itinerary 9*. Trekking Permits are available at the Department of Immigration.

Customs and Airport Tax

If you have brought your bike into Nepal, Customs may indicate this in your passport in which case you must take your bicycle out with you when you leave. A departure tax of Rs 700 is charged on international flights.

Time Differences

Nepal is 5 hours and 45 minutes ahead of GMT and 15 minutes ahead of Indian Standard Time.

GETTING ACQUAINTED

How Not To Offend

Do not rely on Nepalis to tell you whether you are wearing or doing something wrong, or on their friendliness as the measure of the appropriateness of your actions. They are generally too polite to tell you straight. Avoid inadvertently offending your hosts by keeping the following in mind:

– If you are approached or hassled by the curious, smiling patiently usually gets better results than losing your cool.

– Rarely do people mind being photographed, but it is polite to be tactful and stop if they object.

Respect to deities in temples and shrines is expected; be ready to remove your shoes and put on your best behaviour.

The traditional greeting, *'Namaste'* or *'Namaskar'*, should be spoken as a greeting while raising both hands in a prayer-like gesture.

– The King is regarded with genuine reverence as an incarnation of Vishnu, so all references to the royal family must be suitably respectful.

– Never point with a finger and especially not with your feet. Never touch the top of anyone's head and never give or receive anything in your left 'polluted' hand. Best to offer with your right hand and receive with both hands.

– Avoid sharing food or eating and drinking utensils with others, or dipping into the common food bowl with anything that touches your lips.

MONEY MATTERS

Currency

Nepalese rupees are the monetary unit and the official rate of exchange fluctuates against a basket of currencies. At time of press the rate was about Rs 50 to US$1, but check the *Rising Nepal* newspaper where rates are published daily on the back page.

Money can be changed in banks and hotels and there is an exchange counter at the airport. Beware of the black market as hard currency is in high demand. Keep all Foreign Exchange Encashment Receipts as these are necessary for visa extensions and changing back excess rupees on departure. It is illegal to export or import Nepalese currency. Foreigners must make all airline, hotel and travel agency payments in foreign exchange.

American Express, Master Card and Visa credit cards are widely accepted.

Tipping

It is customary, though not mandatory, to tip about 10 percent in restaurants and hotels but not to taxi drivers unless they wait or perform unexpected services. Give Rs 3–5 to a hotel porter who helps with your bags. You may want to give a few rupees to the handicapped or religious mendicants, but please refrain from giving gifts of sweets, pens and money to children.

GETTING AROUND

Traffic

Kathmandu's street traffic, to the newcomer, can seem like a lawless and chaotic affair. There is a sort of order, however, that you should comprehend quickly for greater safety, whether riding, walking or driving. It is the order of the 'biggest and most brash goes first'.

Pedestrians have the lowest status and conversely their approach is one of extreme bravado. They will cross streets without looking to gain the upper hand. Villagers unaccustomed to cars are oblivious to vehicular speed and danger. Bicyclists will turn suddenly or weave across a street without looking. Motorcycles and cars pull out from side streets without looking, cutting you off with little concern. Cars and trucks will pass each other at turns, on hills and when others are approaching from the opposite direction. By virtue of their size, the kings of the road are the Tata trucks and the blue public buses.

Exercise caution: pedestrians and bikers beware, you are the small fish in the pond! Operate defensively, as if the worst situation is about to happen and you will ride and walk safely.

Private Cars

You can have your hotel or travel agent arrange a private car for trips which require a drop-off at a trailhead. This is the simplest but also the most expensive, with average rates of about US$50 per day.

Taxis

Taxis are available for hire to most places and have black registration plates with white numbers. Make sure their meters are working and be prepared to pay a 30 percent fuel surcharge.

You can hail your own taxi on the street and negotiate a fare for a half or full-day to outlying areas. Around town, during the daytime, insist on using the meter, but at night expect to pay 25–50 percent higher. Full-day fares may be approximately Rs 1,200. Make sure that the taxi driver understands where you want to go; show your destination on the map and repeat yourself a few times. Do not pay in advance, pay only when the trip is over. You can give an extra Rs 10 for tea when the driver waits for you.

This method is only recommended if you have learned to enjoy the 'Asian Barter Game'. Example: driver quotes a price, you divide by two and then meet him somewhere in the middle. With a little humour thrown in, it can be fun and the beginning of a good day together.

Public Transport

Buses, trams, three-wheeled scooters (*tempos*) and bicycle rickshaws all ply the streets of Kathmandu.

Carry a small first aid kit with bandage alcohol preps, aspirin, iodine, soap a sunscreen. If you are bitten by a do wash the wound immediately with soa and hot water and consult a doctor as the risk of rabies. Drink lots of water a keep out of the sun if you get overheate If a companion needs emergency medic attention and cannot be moved, you mu take control of the situation as village may not understand this concept. St with your companion and send a no with a reliable person to one of the cli ics or hospitals.

I recommend carrying *The Pocket Do tor* by Stephen Bezruschka, published t The Mountaineers, Seattle, Washingto 1988, for tips on basic health care ar emergencies.

Hygiene

It is not uncommon for minor problem to occur so elementary hygiene preca tions are in order. Never drink unboile and untreated water and do not trust i cubes anywhere except in the best hote Avoid eating raw vegetables, peel all fru and only eat in proper restaurants. Nev walk barefoot and wash your hands ofte 'Travellers Tummy' should clear up aft a couple of days but if it is particular severe and persistent, or interferes wit your travel plans, get a stool test an seek medical assistance.

Medical Services

There are Nepali doctors attached to a the big hotels. The Nepal Internation Clinic (Tel: 412842) is in Naxal and t American-staffed CIWEC Clinic (Te 410983) is in Baluwatar (opposite th Russian Embassy).

Some Kathmandu hospitals have Eng lish-speaking staff but services are not u to international standards. Where feas ble, foreign visitors with serious problem are advised to go to the excellent faciliti in Bangkok, Thailand. For accidents an emergencies, the recommended hospita are the Patan Hospital (Tel: 52103 521048) in Lagankhel, Patan, run by th

United Mission to Nepal and the Teaching Hospital (Tel: 412303, 412404) in Maharajgunj.

Crime

Keep your wallet out of sight and your bag zipped up. Although the Kathmandu Valley is still relatively safe, crime is increasing and I caution women not to walk alone late at night anywhere in the city. Bicycles should not be left unattended even if locked overnight on the street or outside your hotel. Lock your bike to a pole or something stationary at all times when you leave it – mountain bike thefts are not uncommon.

COMMUNICATIONS

Give letters to your hotel desk or take them to the GPO yourself (open 10am–5pm daily except Saturday and holidays). Many hotels, travel agents and commercial communications offices now have international telephone, telefax and telex services. The country code is 977 and the Kathmandu area code is 1. To call other countries first dial the international access code 00, followed by the country code: Australia (61); France (33); Germany (49); Italy (39); Japan (81); Netherlands (31); Spain (34); UK (44); US and Canada (1). US telephone cards are not yet in use here.

FOOD, WATER & NUTRITION

Physical exercise burns up calories that need to be replenished over the course of the exercise. If you wait too long to eat

or drink, you will feel faint. Eating and drinking during exercise can mean the difference between feeling totally beat or invigorated and alive at the end of the day. Here are some suggestions on what and when to eat:

Pre-Trip Meal

Eat a high carbohydrate and low fat meal 1–2 hours before exercise. Pancakes, porridge, french toast, oatmeal, *naan* (local *tandoori* bread), toast with jam, fruit, pasta and rice are ideal foods.

Snacks for the Trip

Cookies, dried fruits, bananas, M&M's, nuts and chocolate bars are available at 'cold stores' throughout Kathmandu. *Chyura* (beaten rice) and fruit can be purchased at some local vegetable markets and in Asan Tole in the old city.

Lunch Foods

Peanut butter and jelly (heavy on the jelly and light on the peanut butter) or honey-banana sandwiches are ideal and better than cheese, tuna or meat as proteins take longer to break down. Rolls, breads, cakes (ie carbohydrates) are good too. Gourmet Delicatessen and Pumpernickel Bakery in Thamel can make a sandwich to go and the German Bakery in town is good for breads, cookies and cakes.

Liquids

The amount you should drink while biking or hiking depends upon your exertion level, speed and air temperature; adjust accordingly. These guidelines are the minimum required.
– Begin drinking no more than 20 minutes after starting the trip, and at every 20-minute intervals drink ¼ to ⅓ litre.
– Do not wait until you are thirsty to drink.
– You can combine eating and drinking.
   Drink suggestions: Gatorade (available at some local supermarkets), Tang (orange powder drink), water, sweetened lemon tea and fruit juices; never beer.

BIKE & HIKE TIPS

We are all used to walking, and biking, to varying degrees, but as hiking and mountain biking in such steep terrain puts exceptional strain on the body, I have suggested some techniques.

Biking

– Do not use your front brake first going downhill; this will surely catapult you over the front handlebars. Use it after you have applied the rear brakes. Brake before going too fast.

– On rough roads and downhills, bend your elbows slightly, keep a soft grip on the handlebars, your pedals horizontal to the road with both knees bent and your weight slightly back off the saddle. Relax your body and let the fat tyres and frame take the bumps.

– Shift to an easier gear before you start climbing a hill and keep your weight balanced between the front and rear tyres.

– If you have to stand on a hill and pedal, which is equivalent to shifting to the next easier gear, keep your weight a bit over the rear tyre for traction.

Pushing

– While pushing your bike, always put the bike on the downhill side of the path.

– At narrow sections, hold the seat with your outside hand and the handlebar with your inside hand and keep the weight off the rear tyre by gently lifting as you push forward.

– When you are half dragging and pulling your bike uphill, push with both hands on the handlebars and let the rear tyre follow.

Carrying

Rule number one is, if you lose your balance, let the bike fall rather than yourself. There are three basic ways to carry a bike:

– Put your shoulder under the top tube where it meets the down tube, just under the seat. Hoist it on your shoulder and keep the handlebars down at knee level. If you must carry it for a long distance, it helps to pad the bar with something soft.

– For long climbs, take the wheels off. Tie them and the frame

to your backpack.

– Pay a local porter to carry your bike the top. This supports the local econom and it's easier on your back!

Walking

– Walk downhill with bent knees as you were about to sit down, and let th thigh muscles do more work. It is easi on the vulnerable knees, although it w give your thighs a real work-out.

– Do not step down with a stiff (hype extended) leg or you may get Sahib knees, a condition that causes extrem pain behind the knee cap. In its wor stage it will incapacitate you.

_ Tie your shoe laces tight when yo know you will be going downhill for long time. It helps prevent blisters.

– Lactic acid builds up in muscles whe you stop after a strenuous work-out, t result being that your legs feel like log To prevent this, take frequent short res (5 minutes) rather than long rests o steep or difficult terrain.

Specialist Attire

The most comfortable clothes for bikin and walking are loose fitting garment layered for temperature changes. Tan tops are improper for both men or wome no matter how hot it is. Men should a ways wear a shirt in public, except for quick douse under the tap to cool off.

It is socially acceptable for men to wea long shorts but strictly *faux pas* fo women. A full skirt or loose pants whic cover the knees even when riding is woman's best bet. A pair of tights unde neath sets you up well, unless it is the h season. For long bike rides, padded lyc biking shorts worn underneath other ga ments prevents chaffing and gives extr cushion to the seat. If you have arrived i Kathmandu without the proper clothin you can purchase inexpensive clothes i Thamel.

Equipment

Always wear a helmet on a mountai bike. Head injury is the leading cause c bike accident deaths and a helmet wi save your life; it's that simple. Many bik

has competent, well-trained guides-cum-mechanics who lead you on all trips, and provide a sag wagon and full camping support services. They provide the bikes (better quality than those available in most rental shops), helmets, water bottle, panniers and arrange all accommodation and food on longer trips. Contact them at:

HIMALAYAN MOUNTAIN BIKES
PO Box 2247, Kathmandu, Nepal
Tel: 411724, Fax: 977-1-415284,
Tlx: 2375 PEACE NP

rental shops will provide helmets and you can rent a climbing helmet at the local trekking shops.

If you already have a case of Sahib's knees, you might pick up a walking stick to help brace yourself on the steep downhill hikes. You can find them in some trekking shops in Thamel, along with second-hand hiking boots and a surprising array of equipment.

The following equipment is recommended for longer bikes and hikes:

– Water bottle (litre/quart)
– Iodine for purifying water
– Wind parka
– Sweater or light pile jacket
– Rain gear (during monsoon months)
– Bike tools, if you have them
– Tube repair kit and pump
– Flashlight, matches and pocket knife

For treks, there are three trekking companies I recommend. They make all arrangements like securing trek permits and providing equipment, Sherpa guides, cooks, food and all the necessary support services for treks into the hills.

CHO-OYU TREKKING
PO Box 4515, Kathmandu, Nepal
Tel: 418890, Fax: 9771-418890,
Tlx: 2276 HOSANG NP

MOUNTAIN TRAVEL NEPAL
PO Box 170, Kathmandu, Nepal
Tel: 414508, 413019, Fax: 9771-414075,
Tlx: 2216 TIGTOP NP

Bike Parts and Rentals

Cheap made-in-Hong Kong parts are available at bike rental shops located near Asan Tole.

Bikes can be rented at four locations in Thamel. Rentals range from Rs 60–200 per day, slightly less per week. Take the bikes out for a test run before heading out of town; make sure the brakes and derailleur are in working order.

MRS RENTAL SERVICE
Tel: 228827 (Shop), 215629 (Home)

NEPAL BY BICYCLE
Tel: 228033, Fax: 222026

YANGRIMA TREKKING
PO Box 2951, Kathmandu, Nepal
Tel: 227627, Fax: 9771-227628,
Tlx: 2474 SUMTR NP

USEFUL INFORMATION

Guide Books and Maps

They are many, but recommended are *Insight Cityguide Kathmandu*, *Insight Guide Nepal* and *Insight Pocket Guide Nepal*, published by APA Publications and widely

Bike Tours and Treks

There is only one mountain bike touring company which I personally recommend. Himalayan Mountain Bikes has organised and led tours in Nepal for 5 years, and available. The informative *Nepal Traveller* magazine may be handed to you at the airport. Erwin Schneider's Kathmandu Valley map is the best and the orange street-map of Kathmandu, published by Himalayan Booksellers, is useful.

There are a number of very good bookshops in Kathmandu with an excellent selection of books about Nepal. These include: Himalayan Booksellers with branches in Durbar Marg, Kantipath, Thamel; Pilgrims Book Centre north from the Kathmandu Guest House; Mandala Book Point in Kantipath; Educational Enterprises in Kantipath opposite Bir Hospital; Himalayan Book Centre in Bagh Bazaar; and the Tibet Book Store in Keshar Mahal near Immigration.

For useful information on how to bike, hike or trek sensitively — ie with respect for the culture and environment — visit KEEP, the Kathmandu Environment Education Project, located in Hotel Tilicho on Tridevi Marg between the Department of Immigration and Thamel (Tel: 412964, open 10am–5pm except Saturday).

Key Telephone Numbers

Police Emergency	226998
Red Cross Ambulance	228094
Patan Hospital	521034, 521048,
	522286, 522278
Teaching Hospital	412303, 412404,
	412505, 412808
CIWEC Clinic	410983
Nepal International Clinic	412842
Fire Brigade	221177
Telephone Enquiries	197
International Operator	186

FURTHER READING

General

A Mountain in Tibet by Charles Allen and Andre Deutsch. A collection of stories of early Asian explorers trying to discover the sacred Mount Kailash.

Insight Pocket Guide: Nepal by Lisa Choegyal, Apa Publications, Singapore 1993. Personal recommendations and more information in the same series.

Nepal: The Kingdom in the Himalayas by Toni Hagen, Berne: Kummerly and Frey,

1980. Geographical study with many photos and maps. One of the best books b one of the first persons to travel widely i Nepal.

Trespassers on the Roof of the World, Th Race to Lhasa by Peter Hopkirk, Oxfor University Press, 1982. Historical ac counts of early adventurers trying to er ter Lhasa.

Kathmandu City on the Edge of The Worl by Thomas L Kelly and Patricia Roberts A beautifully illustrated book on th Kathmandu valley. It takes you throug Kathmandu's historical layers and festi vals.

Hidden Himalayas by Thomas L Kell and Carroll Dunham. Documents the cy cles of the seasons in Humla, the remot far northwest corner of Nepal.

People, Art & Culture

Festivals of Nepal by Mary M Anderson George Allen & Unwin, London, 1971 Comprehensive summary of festivals.

People of Nepal by Dor Bahadur Bist. and Ratna Pustak Bhandar, Kathmandu 1974. A classic survey.

Natural History

Birds of Nepal by R L Fleming Sr, R L Fleming Jr and L S Bangdel, Avalok, Kathmandu, 1979. Definitive work with good illustrations.

Concise Flowers of the Himalaya by Oleg Polunin and Adam Stainton, Oxford University Press, New Delhi, 1987. A much-needed guide with beautiful illustrations.

Enjoy Trees: A Simple Guide to Some of the Shrubs Found in Nepal by Adrian and Jimmy Storrs, Sahayogi Press, Kathmandu, 1987. Useful and practical handbook.

Trekking

The Trekking Peaks of Nepal by Bill O'Connor, Seattle, Cloudcap Press 1989 and England, Crowood Press. Excellent detailed guide with useful maps.

The Nepal Trekker's Handbook by Amy R Kaplan and Michael Keller, Mustang Publishing Co Inc 1989. Concise, witty and enjoyable book about how to organise your trek and what to expect.

Insight Guide Nepal by Hans Höfer and Lisa Choegyal, APA Publications, Singapore 1991. Most complete coverage of trekking, climbing, national parks, the Terai and the Kathmandu Valley.

Trekking in Nepal, West Tibet and Bhutan, by Hugh Swift, Sierra Club, San Francisco, 1989. Good general route information.

GLOSSARY

A

Asadh – The third month of the Nepalese year (June–July).

Ashwin – The sixth month of the Nepalese year (September–October).

Ashta Matrikas – The eight mother goddesses said to attend on Shiva.

B

bahal – A two-storey Buddhist monastery enclosing a courtyard.

Baisakh – The first month of the Nepalese year (April–May).

Bajra Jogini – A Tantric goddess.

betel – A stimulating mixture of araca nut and white lime, wrapped in a leaf and chewed.

Bhadra – The fifth month of the Nepalese year (August–September).

Bhairav – The god Shiva in his most terrifying form.

Bhimsen – A deity worshipped for his strength and courage.

bodhisattva – In Mahayana tradition, a person who has attained but has chosen to remain on earth to teach others.

Brahma – In Hindu mythology, the god of creation.

Brahman – The highest of Hindu castes, originally that of priests.

C

Chaitra – The 12th and last month of the Nepalese year (March–April).

chaitya – A small stupa, sometimes containing a Buddhist relic.

chhang – A potent mountain beer of fermented grain.

Chhetri – The Hindu warrior caste, second in status only to Brahmans.

chiya – Nepalese tea, brewed with milk, sugar and spices.

chorten – A small Buddhist shrine.

chowk – A palace or public courtyard.

D–F

Devi (or Maha Devi) – Shiva's shakti in one of her many forms.

dal – A lentil 'soup'.

dharmasala – A public rest house for travellers and pilgrims.

Durga – Shiva's *shakti* in one of her most awesome forms.

dyochhen – A house for enshrining deities.

Falgun – The 11th month of the Nepalese year (February–March).

G–H

gaine – A wandering, begging minstrel.

Ganesh – The elephant-headed son of Shiva and Parvati.

Garuda – A mythical eagle, half-human; the vehicle of Vishnu.

ghat – A riverside platform for bathing and cremation.

gompa – Tibetan Buddhist monastery.

guthi – A communal Newar brotherhood.

Hanuman – A deified monkey, hero of the Ramayana epic.

hiti – A water conduit; a bath or tank with water spouts.

J–K

jatra – festival.

Jesth – The second month of the Nepalese year (May–June).

Jogini – A mystical goddess.

jyapu – Newar farmer caste.

Kali – Shiva's *shakti* in her most terrifying form.

karma – The cause and effect chain of actions – good and bad – from one life to the next.

Kartik – The seventh month of the

Nepalese year (October–November).

khukri – A traditional knife, long and curved.

Krishna – The eighth incarnation of Vishnu, heavily worshipped for his activities on earth.

kumari – A young virgin regarded as a living goddess in Kathmandu Valley towns.

L

Lakshmi – The goddess of wealth and consort of Vishnu.

lama – A Tibetan Buddhist priest.

lingum – A symbolic male phallus, generally associated with Shiva.

M

Machhendra – The guardian god of the Kathmandu Valley, guarantor of rain and plenty.

Magha – the 10th month of the Nepalese year (January–February).

Mahayana – A form of Buddhism prevalent in East Asia, Tibet and Nepal.

mandala – A sacred diagram envisioned by Tibetan Buddhists as an aid to meditation.

mandap – a roofless Tantric shrine made of brick or wood.

Manjushri – The legendary Buddhist patriarch of Kathmandu.

mantra – Sacred syllables chanted during meditation by Buddhists.

Marga – The eighth month of the Nepalese year (November–December).

math – A Hindu priest's house.

N

naga – A legendary or deified serpent.

Narayan – Vishnu represented as the creator of life.

nirvana – Extinction of self, the goal of meditation.

P

Parvati – Shiva's consort, displaying both serene and fearful aspects.

pashmina – A shawl or blanket made of fine goat's wool.

Pashupati – Shiva in his aspect as Lord of the Beasts.

paathi – A shelter for travellers and pilgrims.

pokhari – A large tank.

Poush – The ninth month of the Nepalese year (December–January).

puja – Ritual offerings to the gods.

R–S

rakshi – A homemade wheat or rice liquor.

Rinpoche – The abbot of a Tibetan Buddhist monastery.

sadhu – A Hindu mendicant.

Saraswati – Brahma's consort, worshipped in Nepal as the Hindu goddess of learning.

shakti – Shiva's consort. Literally, the dynamic element in the male-female relationship, and the female aspect of the Tantric Absolute.

shikhara – A temple of geometrical shape with a tall central spire.

Shiva – The most awesome of Hindu gods. He destroys all things, good as well as evil, allowing new creation to take shape.

Srawan – The fourth month of the Nepalese year (July–August).

stupa – A bell-shaped relic chamber.

T–U

thangka – A religious scroll painting.

tole – A street.

V–Z

vajra – In Tantric Buddhism, a ritual thunderbolt or curved sceptre symbolising the Absolute (also *dorje*).

Vishnu – One of the Hindu trinity, a god who preserves life and the world itself.

yoni – A hole in a stone symbolising the female sexual aspect.

Index

ACKNOWLEDGMENTS

Cover Photography	James Giambrone
Pages 12, 13T, 15, 20, 25, 40, 42T, 42B, 44, 49T, 51T, 51B, 53, 55B, 58B, 59B, 60, 61T, 61B, 63B, 67T, 81T, 82B, 83, 85T, 88T, 92T	James Giambrone
5, 18B, 20T, 22B, 31T, 33T, 37T, 55T, 64B, 68T, 68B, 75, 86B, 102, 105	Lindel Caine
6/7, 10/11, 18T, 21, 22T, 26B, 27, 28, 29T, 29B, 30B, 31B, 32B, 34T, 35B, 41T, 52, 54, 56, 57T, 65, 70T, 74, 76, 77T, 78T, 78B, 81B, 92B, 99T, 103T, 103B, 107B	Thomas L Kelly
13B, 16, 19, 30T, 36T, 36B, 80B, 91	Gary McCue
23, 24T, 41B, 43, 57B, 60T, 63T, 64T, 72, 80T, 87, 89, 90, 94T, 94B, 97T, 97B, 98, 99B, 100T,100B, 106	Wendy B Lama
24B, 45T, 47, 48, 50T, 62, 69, 84, 88B, 95, 96, 101	Jock Montgomery
26T, 93	Arlene Burns
32T, 37B, 49B, 58T, 66B, 82T	Hans Höfer
33B	Thomas Laird
35T, 59T	Alain Evrard
39	Bill Wassman
38, 104, 107	Pradeep Yonzon
46T	David Messent
46B, 79	Frances Klatzel
66T	GP Reichelt
70B, 71, 73B	S Presern
73T	Belinda Edwards
77B	Chuck McDougal
85B, 86T	Sanu R Vajracharya
Handwriting	V Barl
Cover Design	Klaus Geisler
Cartography	Berndtson & Berndtson